RO

Stage number	Title					
1	Lucca to Altopa					
2	Altopascio to San Miniato	28.7km	537m	410m	7¾hr	44
3	San Miniato to Gambassi Terme	24.1km	820m	639m	7hr	52
4	Gambassi Terme to San Gimignano	13.7km	476m	468m	4hr	58
5	San Gimignano to Monteriggioni	27.4km (or 30.9km)	719m (or 753m)	777m (or 812m)	7¾hr	63
6	Monteriggioni to Siena	20.6km	514m	456m	5¾hr	72
7	Siena to Ponte d'Arbia	25.9km	391m	572m	7hr	81
8	Ponte d'Arbia to San Quirico d'Orcia	26.2km	807m	541m	7½hr	88
9	San Quirico d'Orcia to Radicofani	32.9km	1164m	790m	9¾hr	94
10	Radicofani to Acquapendente	23.1km (or 31.3km)	392m (or 708m)	801m (or 1117m)	6¼hr	104
11	Acquapendente to Bolsena	23.2km	503m	564m	6½hr	113
12	Bolsena to Montefiascone	16.4km	638m	356m	5½hr	119
13	Montefiascone to Viterbo	18.1km	247m	515m	4¾hr	124
14	Viterbo to Vetralla	16.8km	340m	363m	4½hr	132
15	Vetralla to Sutri	24.0km	475m	511m	6½hr	138
16	Sutri to Campagnano di Roma	27.7km (or 24.5km)	513m	538m	7½hr	145
17	Campagnano di Roma to La Storta	24.2km (or 23.3km)	559m	669m	6¾hr	151
18	La Storta to Vatican City	19.2km	409m	550m	5½hr	157
TOTAL		**410.5km**	**9689m**	**9709m**	**115hr**	

This book is dedicated to my amazing granddaughter, Frankie,
a constant joy and wonder since the day she was born.

Acknowledgments

Many people helped push this series out into the world. Jonathan and Joe Williams at Cicerone graciously gave it the nod at the start, then the talented Cicerone Team took over once the manuscript landed on their desks. Andrea Grimshaw contributed wise and careful edits, while John Bingley skillfully edited the maps. Raffaele Mannelli and his colleagues at the Regione Toscana gave important guidance and contacts. Rebecca Winke was my lifeline in an emergency. Dear friends at Comitato Linguistico in Perugia helped me through my first steps in the Italian language. Contacts and advice were always joyfully offered by Gigi Bettin. It was a pleasure to work with Luca Bruschi and Sami Tawfik of the European Association of Vie Francigene. Along the way many pilgrim friends broke up the solitude with friendship and laughter, while my wife, Theresa Elliott, walked with me many over delightful kilometers.

WALKING THE VIA FRANCIGENA

PART 3

LUCCA TO ROME

by Sandy Brown

JUNIPER HOUSE, MURLEY MOSS,
OXENHOLME ROAD, KENDAL, CUMBRIA LA9 7RL
www.cicerone.co.uk

© Sandy Brown 2021
First edition 2021
ISBN: 978 1 78631 079 8

Printed in China on responsibly sourced paper on behalf of Latitude Press Ltd.
A catalogue record for this book is available from the British Library.
All photographs are by the author unless otherwise stated.

Route mapping by Lovell Johns www.lovelljohns.com
Contains OpenStreetMap.org data © OpenStreetMap contributors, CC-BY-SA. NASA relief data courtesy of ESRI

Updates to this guide

While every effort is made by our authors to ensure the accuracy of guidebooks as they go to print, changes can occur during the lifetime of an edition. This guidebook was researched and written before the COVID-19 pandemic. While we are not aware of any significant changes to routes or facilities at the time of printing, it is likely that the current situation will give rise to more changes than would usually be expected. Any updates that we know of for this guide will be on the Cicerone website (www.cicerone.co.uk/1079/updates), so please check before planning your trip. We also advise that you check information about such things as transport, accommodation and shops locally. Even rights of way can be altered over time.

We are always grateful for information about any discrepancies between a guidebook and the facts on the ground, sent by email to updates@cicerone.co.uk or by post to Cicerone, Juniper House, Murley Moss, Oxenholme Road, Kendal, LA9 7RL.

Register your book: To sign up to receive free updates, special offers and GPX files where available, register your book at www.cicerone.co.uk.

Front cover: Cypress trees frame two pilgrims between Buonconvento and San Quirico d'Orcia (Stage 8)

CONTENTS

Route summary table 1
Map key 7
Overview profile Lucca to Rome 8
Foreword 11

INTRODUCTION: THE VIA FRANCIGENA FROM LUCCA TO ROME 13
A brief history of the Via Francigena 14
Sigeric and the modern Via Francigena 16

PLANNING YOUR WALK 18
Where to begin 18
When to walk 18
Where to stay 18
What and where to eat 19
Should I make reservations ahead? 20
How much money should I budget? 21
How do I get to this portion of the Via Francigena? 21
How do I return from Rome? 23
How do I secure my credential and Testimonium? 23

TIPS FOR MAKING THE MOST OF YOUR WALK 25
Topography of the Via Francigena in Central Italy 25
Understanding local cultures 25
Training for your walk 26
What and how to pack 26
Baggage transport and storage 27
Health and well-being 28

HOW TO USE THIS GUIDE 29
Route descriptions 29
GPX tracks and accommodation downloads 32

SECTION 1: TUSCANY 33
Stage 1   Lucca to Altopascio 36
Stage 2   Altopascio to San Miniato 44
Stage 3   San Miniato to Gambassi Terme 52
Stage 4   Gambassi Terme to San Gimignano 58
Stage 5   San Gimignano to Monteriggioni 63

Stage 6   Monteriggioni to Siena 72
Stage 7   Siena to Ponte d'Arbia. 81
Stage 8   Ponte d'Arbia to San Quirico d'Orcia 88
Stage 9   San Quirico d'Orcia to Radicofani 94
Stage 10   Radicofani to Acquapendente 104

SECTION 2: LAZIO 111
Stage 11   Acquapendente to Bolsena 113
Stage 12   Bolsena to Montefiascone 119
Stage 13   Montefiascone to Viterbo 124
Stage 14/15 Cimino Variant: Viterbo to Sutri 130
Stage 14   Viterbo to Vetralla 132
Stage 15   Vetralla to Sutri 138
Stage 16   Sutri to Campagnano di Roma. 145
Stage 17   Campagnano di Roma to La Storta 151
Stage 18   La Storta to Vatican City 157

Appendix A   Stage planning table. 166
Appendix B   Useful contacts. 168
Appendix C   Bibliography. 170
Appendix D   Sigeric's journey: then and now 171

A Via Francigena guide in three parts 176
Map of the Via Francigena Canterbury to Rome 177
Profile of the Via Francigena Canterbury to Rome. 178

Note on mapping

The route maps in this guide are derived from publicly available data, databases and crowd-sourced data. As such they have not been through the detailed checking procedures that would generally be applied to a published map from an official mapping agency. However, we have reviewed them closely in the light of local knowledge as part of the preparation of this guide.

Symbols used on maps

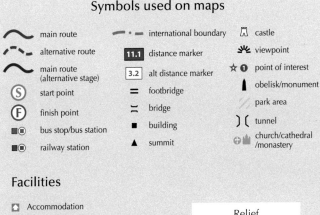

∼ main route	⚊·⚊ international boundary	🏰 castle
⚊ alternative route	**11.1** distance marker	🌿 viewpoint
∼ main route (alternative stage)	3.2 alt distance marker	☆ ❶ point of interest
Ⓢ start point	= footbridge	▌ obelisk/monument
Ⓕ finish point	≈ bridge	park area
■◉ bus stop/bus station	■ building	) (tunnel
■◉ railway station	▲ summit	⊕ 🏛 church/cathedral /monastery

Facilities

- 🏠 Accommodation
  - 🏠 ostello (hostel)
  - 🏠 hotel
  - 🏠 camere (rooms)
  - 🏠 B&B
  - 🏠 agriturismo
- 🏕 ▲ camping

- 🍴 Catering
  - 🍷 bar
  - 🍽 restaurant
  - ☕ café

- ⊕ groceries
- 🚻 public toilets
- 🏧 ATM
- 💧 drinking water tap
- 🪑 rest/picnic area
- ⊕ pharmacy
- Ⓗ hospital
- ⊕ medical clinic
- ❶ tourist/pilgrim information

Relief
in meters

800–1000
600–800
400–600
200–400
0–200

MAP SCALES
Route maps at 1:100,000
Town maps at 1:25,000 unless
otherwise stated (see scale bar)

SCALE: 1:100,000

0 kilometres 1   2
0 miles   1

SCALE: 1:25,000

0 kilometres 0.25   0.5
0 miles   0.25

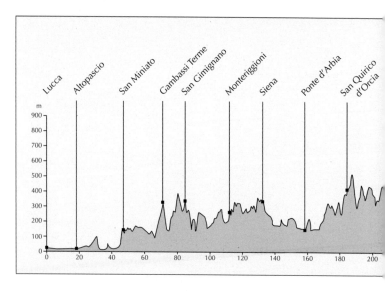

The town of Montalcino towers above vineyards of prestigious Brunello wines (Stage 8)

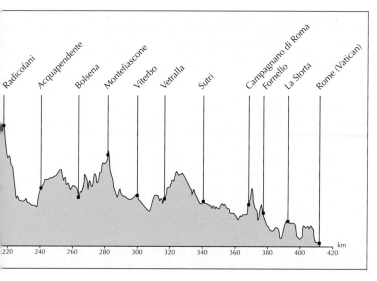

L to R: Palazzo Comunale, Torre Grossa and the Duomo Collegiate Church in Piazza del Duomo of San Gimignano (Stage 4)

FOREWORD

The Via Francigena – Road to Rome – was designated a Cultural Route by the Council of Europe in 1994. The European Association of Via Francigena Ways (EAVF) is a voluntary association of regions and local authorities in England, France, Switzerland and Italy, which currently has more than 180 members. It was established on 7 April 2001 in Fidenza (Italy) to promote the Via Francigena – 3200km (2000 miles) from Canterbury to Rome and, in the Via Francigena del Sud (certified since 2019), to Santa Maria di Leuca.

The route travels from Canterbury in the UK through France and Switzerland to Rome, and continues to the south of Italy, heading towards Jerusalem. It passes through 16 European regions (Kent; Hauts-de-France; Grand Est; Bourgogne-Franche-Comté; Vaud; Valais; Valle d'Aosta; Piedmont; Lombardy; Emilia-Romagna; Liguria; Tuscany; Lazio; Campania, Basilicata, Apulia) in four countries (UK; France; Switzerland; Italy). The association carries out activities to enhance and promote the route at all institutional levels: local, regional, national and European. In 2007 the Council of Europe declared the EAVF the Lead Agency of the Via Francigena, assigning it the role of official reference point for safeguarding, protecting, promoting and developing the Via Francigena in Europe.

This guide to the Via Francigena from Lucca to Rome is the result of collaboration between the EAVF, Cicerone Press and local associations. It is aimed at walkers and pilgrims who want to discover the beauty of the Italian section of this historic European route between the superb landscapes of Tuscany and the eternal city of Rome. This is a journey to the heart of Europe, a fascinating way to encounter its traditions, cultural heritage and art treasures while getting to know new people.

The Via Francigena was defined as a 'bridge of cultures between Anglo-Saxon Europe and Latin Europe' by the famous medievalist Jacques Le Goff. The Via Francigena of the third millennium is a path of peace, tolerance and dialogue between cultures, religions and countries.

We wish you all a good journey! *Buon viaggio!*

European Association of Via Francigena Ways (EAVF)
For information, visit www.viefrancigene.org, or follow us on social media:
Facebook: @ViaFrancigenaCulturalRoute   Instagram: viafrancigena_aevf

Two pilgrims make their way toward Bagno Vignoni in morning sunlight (Stage 9)

INTRODUCTION: THE VIA FRANCIGENA
FROM LUCCA TO ROME

While every step of the Via Francigena speaks with its own voice, the final 400km from Lucca to Rome speaks with the most Italian accent. By the time the Via Francigena finds Tuscany at Lucca it is in the heartland of Italy – it was the Tuscan dialect that gave birth to modern Italian, here the Renaissance was born, and here many of Italy's most amazing frescoes, statues and paintings can be admired. The colors which inspired that artistic explosion are visible in the landscape – raw sienna, burnt sienna, sepia, gold, deep greens and vermillion blue – colors that entrance tourists and locals alike.

The Tuscan portion of the Via Francigena crosses through two of the region's most important cities – Lucca and Siena – each with tales to tell about their rivalries with neighbors Florence and Pisa and each worthy of extra time for exploration. As if Lucca and Siena aren't enough, the track also winds its way through San Gimignano, widely recognized as one of the best-preserved medieval towns in Italy, Monteriggioni with its remarkable medieval walls, San Miniato home to an iconic tower and cloistered convent, San Quirico d'Orcia with its medieval churches, and Radicofani known for its mountaintop fortress and legends of bandit heroes.

If Tuscany is the heart of Italy, Lazio is its soul. The Vatican City and Rome are the center of the world's largest religion, after all, and the 900 churches of this city each have a story to tell of saints and martyrs, of holy ones and hypocrites who've colored Christianity's 20 centuries. A Via Francigena pilgrim walks to the Eternal City in the footsteps of Charlemagne, Willibald, Winibald, Nikolás Bergsson of Iceland, Philip Augustus of France, Martin Luther, and of course Sigeric the Serious, 10th c. Archbishop of Canterbury.

There are so many sights to enjoy, like Piazza Anfiteatro in **Lucca**, one of the most picturesque places to sip a cappuccino on the entire Via Francigena. Stop at Lucca's San Martino Cathedral to view the Volto Santo and run your finger along the labyrinth carving at the right portico. Climb the Tower of Federico II in **San Miniato** and enjoy vast views of the surrounding countryside. Book ahead to see the frescoed interior of the Collegiate Church in **San Gimignano**, one of the most colorful in Italy. Walk atop the walls of **Monteriggioni** and imagine you're standing guard as a medieval soldier. No visit to **Siena** is complete without at least an hour inside the amazing Duomo. It's a stiff hike up to the top of the fort at

Radicofani, but the views are unsurpassed. In Lazio, make certain to pay a euro to turn on the lights so you can see the 1000-year-old crypt at the Basilica Cattedrale of San Sepolcro in **Acquapendente**. If weather permits, a refreshing dip in the **Lago di Bolsena** is free of charge. On the next day see the lake from the Rocca dei Papi in **Montefiascone** with its azure and emerald vista. Admission to the relaxing Bagnaccio hot springs before **Viterbo** is free to pilgrims, and the park is right on the trail. Take the time to tour the Ancient City of **Sutri** and the Roman amphitheater there. Walk up the glass steps at the Ostello Maripara in **Formello** to see names of important cities on the Via Francigena and remember your walk.

If you've never been, plan at least two days to enjoy **Rome and the Vatican City**: St Peter's Basilica and the Vatican Museum on the first day and the Ancient Rome of the Pantheon, Coliseum and Forum on the second. In between, relax among the sun-dappled piazzas and splashing fountains. Try dinner and a stroll in Trastevere and toss a coin into the Trevi Fountain, which legends promise will bring you back to visit this amazing city once again.

A BRIEF HISTORY OF THE VIA FRANCIGENA

Newly appointed as Archbishop of Canterbury in 990, Bishop Sigeric of Ramsbury set out to see the Pope and receive his *pallium*, the simple

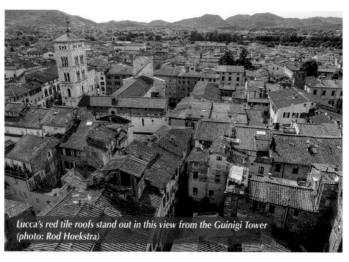

Lucca's red tile roofs stand out in this view from the Guinigi Tower (photo: Rod Hoekstra)

St Peter's Basilica towers above the buildings of Rome and the Vatican

woolen cloak embroidered with a cross that signified both his ascension to archbishop and his allegiance to Rome. While today we might want to think of Sigeric as a hero or pioneer, history remembers him as a fairly undistinguished church leader doing a relatively routine errand of church business while walking a relatively well-trod route journeying down a spoke in the wheel toward the hub of Rome, capital of Western Christianity.

Ancient Rome had established an overland link to Britannia some 1200 years prior in order to speed its conquest of these islands rich in silver, copper, tin and lead. Evangelists traveled in both directions on the route after the fall of Rome, spreading the gospel to the British Isles and then back from Britain and Ireland into the northern reaches

of the Italian peninsula. Pilgrims like Fridianus of Ulster, Richard of Wessex and his sons Winibald and Wilibald headed south to Rome and then beyond Rome to Jerusalem in the 6th–8th c. By the time of Sigeric's journey in the 10th c. there was an Anglo-Saxon residential enclave in Rome – the *Schola Saxonum* – where British and Irish pilgrims made their homes in Rome.

Sigeric's notes, probably an afterthought for him, propelled him into the history books. The archbishop concisely documented the churches he had visited in Rome and then his overnight stops on his trip home. A lettered and cultured man, he donated his papers to Canterbury Cathedral where scribes maintained them, copying parts that were in need of preservation. His papers ultimately made their way to the archives of the British Library where scholars discovered the itinerary of his Roman holiday. A millennium later, this simple two-page manuscript documented a nearly 2000km route, buried in time, that once connected England to Rome. See Appendix D for a translation of the route and its correlation to modern locations.

SIGERIC AND THE MODERN VIA FRANCIGENA

While scholars studied Sigeric's route as early as the late-19th century, it was in 1985 that Italian historian Giovanni Caselli surveyed the entire itinerary from Canterbury to Rome. He brought technicians of the Italian Military Geographical Institute to map the route and at the 1000-year anniversary in 1990 published his guidebook *Via Romea: Cammino di Dio*.

Aiming to make a viable, modern pilgrim route to Rome in anticipation of the 2000 Year of Jubilee, the Italian Ministry of Tourism pulled together regions and local governments along the route to collaborate in building a suitable pilgrim infrastructure, and in 1994 the Via Francigena was recognized as an official 'Cultural Route of the Council of Europe.' This epic walk was now ready to be rediscovered by pilgrims looking for history, adventure and inspiration.

The 11th c. manuscript containing Sigeric's itinerary in Rome and from Rome to the English Channel (courtesy of the British Library)

Vineyards mark the territory near Casanuova (Stage 4)

PLANNING YOUR WALK

Careful planning is key to a smooth pilgrim walk. Here are some tips to consider as you make your preparations. Go to Appendix A for a helpful stage planning guide that lists intermediate distances between pilgrim accommodations.

WHERE TO BEGIN

The Via Francigena officially begins in Canterbury, but not everyone has available the 80–100 days it takes to complete the whole route. Since the minimum distance required of walkers for a completion certificate – or Testimonium – is 100km (200km for cyclists), some people start at Acquapendente, Montefiascone or Viterbo. The most popular starting places on this stretch are Lucca, Sienna and Viterbo. For distances between the towns, see Appendix A.

WHEN TO WALK

Italy's hot summers usually reach their temperature peak around mid-July, with the heat cooling slowly through early September. With that in mind, it's best to avoid walking this stretch in July and August. Spring is an excellent season to walk, with Tuscany's rolling grain fields in their full green glory. Autumn brings the grape and hazelnut harvests and

cool temperatures, making it a good choice, too. Winter hiking on the Via Francigena between Lucca and Rome is very possible given the relatively low elevations involved. Watch, though, for swollen streams and more frequent rain along with shorter daylight hours.

WHERE TO STAY

The Via Francigena between Lucca and Rome offers many accommodation options, with choices suitable for most any budget.

Hostels
The EAVF has done an excellent job of pulling together an infrastructure of low-cost hostels (Italian: *ostello* or plural, *ostelli*) at each planned overnight between Lucca and Rome, sometimes related to religious or volunteer organizations and sometimes to municipalities. Many hostels are *donativo*, which actually means a donation of around €10 is expected. A blanket and pillow are generally provided for use on bunk beds in dormitory rooms with shared bathrooms.

Hotels, B&Bs and camere
Some pilgrims will pay more for the assurance of a reservation and the comfort of bed linens, and hotels and B&Bs are more likely to have

Formello's 11th c. Palazzo Chigi houses the local archeological museum and the town's pilgrim hostel

an online reservation system available and more comfortable amenities. Both generally provide breakfast but expect the extra services to cost you around €50–70 per night. Italian locals also rent rooms – *camere* – which may be in an independent house or in the host's own apartment and may include access to a kitchen for self-catering.

Agriturismi

An *agriturismo* is a farm authorized by the Italian government to provide overnight stays. These dot the rural countryside throughout the walk and most also provide breakfast or both dinner and breakfast (half-board). Costs can vary greatly, but accommodations are usually hotel-like, with comfortable beds, linens and private bathrooms.

Camping

Camping is allowed in Italy only in designated campgrounds in public parks, in private campgrounds, or with permission of a private landowner. There are some private campgrounds near the Via Francigena in Tuscany and Lazio, but often pilgrims who brought along camping gear for early stages of the Via Francigena send their gear back home by the time they arrive in Tuscany due to the ample supply of low-cost hostels.

WHAT AND WHERE TO EAT

Italians are justly proud of their cuisine, and great care is usually taken in preparation of meals.

Via Francigena pilgrims will often find themselves at restaurants where, following the Italian custom, traditional menus are organized by *antipasti* (appetizer), *primi* (first courses, usually pasta), *secondi* (second courses, usually meat) and *dolci* (desserts). Only occasionally is there a set-price pilgrim menu (*menu del Pellegrino*) available.

Pizzerias also dot the urban landscape. Often with a *forno a legno* (wood-fired oven) that adds a wood-smoke flavor and crispy crust to the pie, these are usually sit-down restaurants that produce meal-sized, thin-crust pizzas.

Italian breakfasts are commonly eaten on the run, standing up at a café to drink a quick *cappuccino* (espresso coffee with steamed milk and milk foam) and perhaps eat a *cornetto* (croissant) or *brioche* (muffin or sweet bread). Breakfasts at a hotel might add cheese, fruit, juice and cereal.

In the afternoons for lunch, restaurants are generally still closed, but cafés are usually willing to make a *panino* (sandwich) of *prosciutto crudo* (cured but uncooked ham), *prosciutto cotto* (cured and cooked ham), and/or *formaggio* (cheese) and *pomodoro* (tomato). Setting out in the morning, a good strategy is to ask at your breakfast café for a *panino da portare via*, a sandwich for takeaway or 'to go'. Another strategy is to find a market near your evening destination and buy food for the next day's lunch.

SHOULD I MAKE RESERVATIONS AHEAD?

With a long-distance walk there is always danger in making reservations too far ahead. If your

The castle of Bolsena sits in the foreground while the skyline of Montefiascone stands above (Stage 11)

itinerary is interrupted – by illness, injury, weather, or new friendships – your plans and your reservations can go awry. It's also no fun to be dragged ahead by advance reservations made from home without a clear understanding of the itinerary. A couple of days' advance reservations is best, keeping you flexible in case of anything unforeseen.

Though a few hostels will not accept reservations, it's most always best to call ahead for a hostel bed in Italy. Some hostels will even ask you to call back on the day of your arrival so they don't have to write down your name. Many have no email address or website, which can be frustrating for pilgrims who prefer to lock down their overnight stays online in advance. A common practice is to call the afternoon before the day of your arrival and ask for a reservation. At quieter hostels, call again when you arrive so the host can come and unlock the facility. Keep in mind that the Via Francigena is a favorite trail of local Italian walkers, who can fill pilgrim hostels on weekends, so plan further ahead for Friday and Saturday nights in the summer and during Italian holidays.

HOW MUCH MONEY SHOULD I BUDGET?

The strong network of pilgrim hostels in this stretch of the Via Francigena offers many options for an economical trip. Here's a sample low-end daily budget:

- Hostel lodging donation €10 (€20 with dinner)
- Breakfast (included)
- Sack lunch (packed lunch) €5
- Afternoon snack €5
- Dinner €15 (if not included with lodging)
- Incidentals €5
- Total €35–40 per day

Add more for the occasional glass of wine or beer, for hotel overnights, for more elaborate dinners, for museum admission fees, and other incidentals.

HOW DO I GET TO THIS PORTION OF THE VIA FRANCIGENA?

If not approaching this portion of the route on foot, international pilgrims most commonly fly to Italy, using Rome's Fiumicino Airport as a hub. Once in Italy you can fly to a smaller, regional airport or take a train from the Rome airport to get to your destination. Schedules, prices and reservations are available at www.trenitalia.com (go to www.viefrancigene.org/en/trenitalia for information about how to secure a discount with your official Via Francigena credential). Prices listed below are subject to change and are rounded up to the next full euro amount. Ticket machines at train stations require either cash or a credit/debit card with PIN code. Always endorse your rail ticket at the station's white and green timestamp machine before boarding your train.

The 14th c. Torre del Mangia towers 102m above Siena's central Piazza del Campo

To Lucca or Siena

International airports at Pisa or Florence offer the closest options to these two starting points. From Pisa airport, take the PisaMover shuttle train to Pisa Centrale station (€5, www.pisa-mover.com/en), then pick up the train to Lucca (€4, 30min) or Siena (€11, 1¾hr). From Florence airport, take the VolainBus (€6, departures every 30min) to the Santa Maria Novella train station and from there catch the train to Lucca (€8–11, 1¾hr) or Siena (€10, 1¾hr). From Rome FCO airport, take the express train to Termini station (€14, 30min) and then on to Lucca (€27–44, 3½–5½hr) or Siena (€18–43, 3½–4½hr), both of which will require one transfer. Lucca's historic center is just a 5min walk from the train station via Porta San Pietro. Access to Siena from its train station, which is downhill in the NW section of town, is easiest through a series of escalators at the Galeria PortaSiena that land you a few blocks from the Porta Camollia entrance to the old city, right on the Via Francigena route.

To Montefiascone, Acquapendente, Bolsena or Viterbo

From Rome FCO airport, take the 30min regional train to Roma Ostiense station (€8, every 20min). From there, catch the train to Viterbo Porta Romana station (€6, 2hr). For Montefiascone, Bolsena or Acquapendente catch the Cotral bus from Viterbo (via San Lorenzo Nuovo)

The dome of the Basilica of Santa Margherita dominates the skyline of Montefiascone

(€5, 3 departures daily, https://servizi.cotralspa.it). From Florence airport, take the VolainBus (€6, twice-hourly departures) to Santa Maria Novella train station and from there catch the train to Viterbo Porta Fiorentina station (€19, 4hr) and buses from there to the other towns as noted above.

HOW DO I RETURN FROM ROME?

After finishing your pilgrimage and enjoying the Eternal City, the most common way to return home is by air through Rome's Fiumicino Airport. Local rules require taxis to serve the airport from Central Rome at a fixed price of €48, but less expensive options are the €14 Leonardo Express

train from Termini Station or the local €8 FL1 trains from Trastevere, Ostiense, Tuscolana or Tiburtina stations.

HOW DO I SECURE MY CREDENTIAL AND TESTIMONIUM?

Pilgrim credential:
The pilgrim credential (*credenziale*) is a document that certifies the bearer is a pilgrim who is walking, biking or riding horseback. It allows pilgrims to stay in overnight pilgrim lodging and, if stamped for at least the last 100km before Rome, qualifies the bearer to receive a Testimonium completion certificate at the Vatican in Rome. To

23

The Via Francigena credential

be certain you have it at the start of your walk, it's best to order your credential in advance. The EAVF offers credentials with space enough for the Italian portion of the Via Francigena through its partner SloWays at www. viefrancigene.org/en (€5 plus shipping, allow 1–2 months for delivery). Appendix B contains a list of locations on the Via Francigena where you can collect a credential in person. Plan to hunt down one stamp (*timbro*) corresponding to each overnight along the way. This is usually done at lodgings, but stamps can also be secured at many bars, churches, museums, tourist offices and city halls.

The Testimonium

The Vatican offers pilgrims who have completed a minimum walking distance of 100km an official Testimonium through the busy offices of the Opera Romana Pellegrinaggi just off Saint Peter's Square at Piazza Pio XII, 9 in Rome (09:00–17:00 Mon–Sat, 09:00–13:00 Sun). At present pilgrims are merged with tourists at this sometimes-crowded facility that also sells tickets and tours of Roman holy places. Staff members at the Sacristy inside St Peter's Basilica often have a stack of blank credentials as well. Inside Vatican City security, the offices of the Rectory of St Peters (Petriano entrance on south side of St Peter's, closed Wed and Sun) will also provide a neatly printed Testimonium.

TIPS FOR MAKING THE MOST OF YOUR WALK

TOPOGRAPHY OF THE VIA FRANCIGENA IN CENTRAL ITALY

With the exception of the long, uphill walk to Radicofani, the Via Francigena between Lucca and Rome is best described as gently hilly. Lucca sits at about 25m elevation, as does Rome, so the walk's profile looks like a long slow and bouncy climb to its highest point at Radicofani – also its approximate halfway point – and then a long downhill walk to Rome. Of course, Italy is a country of hilltop towns, so the morning often begins with a downhill walk and the afternoon ends with an uphill climb.

UNDERSTANDING LOCAL CULTURES

Italian culture is diverse, with many regional differences. Still, there are some aspects of Italian culture that are widely shared throughout the country. These quickly become visible to visitors:

The riposo – Pilgrims are often surprised to find Italian streets empty in the afternoon. This is the Italian *riposo*, or 'rest,' in which everything grinds to a halt. Bakeries, restaurants, offices and businesses are generally closed between approximately 12:30 and 16:30 for a long lunch break, rest and family time. Rather than fight it,

Morning mists highlight distant ridges along the trail near San Gimignano

pilgrims are wise to get used to the idea that during this part of the day the only thing open will likely be the local bar and larger shops like supermarkets. If you're not personally observing the *riposo*, that makes the mid-afternoon an excellent time to lounge at a street side café or do your grocery shopping for the next day.

Late breakfasts and later dinners – No matter how much pilgrims may want to leave at the crack of dawn, it's general practice that breakfast comes at about 07:30 or 08:00 each morning. If you want an earlier departure, be sure to notify your hosts. In larger towns there will generally be one café or bakery that opens early in the morning, but in smaller towns (e.g. Monteriggioni), people hoping for an early start will have to either pack their breakfast ahead or wait until the cafés open at 08:00. For evening dinner, restaurants generally open at 19:30pm, which means that a pilgrim who wants to be in bed by 21:00 will have to sleep on a full stomach.

The passeggiata – It is traditional for residents to head out in the evening, particularly on Sundays and holidays, for a relaxing stroll on one of the main shopping streets of town, leading through piazzas and sometimes urban parks. The *passeggiata* is a social time when much of the town turns out and to see friends, breathe in some air in the cool of the evening, and enjoy a gelato or two.

TRAINING FOR YOUR WALK

While anyone who is of average or better fitness can complete a walk of this kind, the experience is much more pleasant with some advance training. Training prepares the muscles and tendons of your legs and feet for the daily regime of long walks and gives you time to fix any shoe or sock problems that might lead to painful blisters.

For a person of average fitness, a training program should include walks of increasing distance over varied terrain for 2–3 months in advance of your trip, building toward at least two successive walks during the week prior to your departure of around 20–25km. Legs and feet strengthened by this kind of training will be less painful after the first few days of walking, which means more fun for you and your companions.

If blisters develop in training walks, adjust the socks and shoes, sandals or boots you are using. Try to duplicate the conditions of your pilgrimage by walking with a loaded pack on varied terrain during training, which benefits cardio conditioning and duplicates the stresses your feet will undergo as you walk in Italy.

WHAT AND HOW TO PACK

Many who walk the Via Francigena have already walked a major pilgrimage route in Europe, perhaps one of the Camino de Santiago itineraries. These experienced walkers already have their packing lists and need little advice, knowing the rule of thumb that a fully loaded pack should weigh in at less than 10% of a pilgrim's body weight, give or take adjustments for very small or very large people.

A good packing list includes:

- Backpack: 35–40 litres
- Clothes: layers, max 2–3 pants and shirts
- Rain gear: poncho, rain jacket or trekking umbrella
- Sun gear: sun hat, sunscreen, sunglasses
- Bedding: hostels are generally equipped with wool blankets, so take a sleeping bag liner in summer, and a lightweight sleeping bag otherwise
- Walking shoes and camp shoes (for around town)
- Hydration system – reusable bottles or bladder
- Basic first-aid kit and blister kit
- Toiletries
- Hiking towel
- Smartphone/camera and charger
- Travel and identity documents
- Debit and credit cards
- Toilet paper and a few plastic bags
- Trekking poles as needed
- Miscellaneous: zippered mesh bags are helpful for keeping your items organized inside your pack. Some like to bring along a small clothesline and clothespins for drying just-washed items as well as earplugs for a restful sleep.

A steel pilgrim statue stands below the Rocca dei Papi in Montefiascone

BAGGAGE TRANSPORT AND STORAGE

Baggage transport service is available from Lucca to Rome through SloWays (€15/ea, info@sloways. eu) and BagsFree (€20, francigena@ bags-free.com). BagsFree also offers a baggage storage service near Rome's Termini train station (www.bags-free. com). Transport from Viterbo to Rome is available through Via-Francigena-Viterbo-Roma (www.viafrancigena-viterbo-roma.it). See Appendix B for more information.

Pilgrims walking through the narrow streets of Acquapendente (Stages 10 and 11)

HEALTH AND WELL-BEING

Italy has a state-of-the-art national telephone system to contact ambulance and police, with English-speaking operators available 24/7 to answer emergency calls.

Emergency phone numbers: –

- 112 Carabinieri – this alerts the national police and is a general emergency number that will route you to the appropriate agency
- 113 State police – theft, robbery, assaults, accidents and health emergencies
- 115 Fire department
- 117 Finance police (if you've been cheated in a retail transaction)
- 118 Medical emergencies – this is the best number to call if you have a health-related emergency and need an ambulance or emergency room
- 1515 Forest fires

If you become sick or injured and don't feel it's an emergency, a good starting place for information is the local pharmacy, which is marked in Italy with the sign of a green cross above the storefront. If he or she can't help you, the pharmacist will recommend a nearby clinic (Guardia Medica) or hospital. Your overnight host is a valuable source of information about local transportation, clinics, hospitals and doctors.

HOW TO USE THIS GUIDE

As part of Cicerone's pilgrimage series, this guidebook is specifically designed with your walk in mind. Since the main body of research for the guide was completed, the world has been struck by the COVID-19 virus. It is likely that facilities and accommodation will be affected by this pandemic for some time after publication. We have checked information as close to publication date as practicable, but please do let us know of any serious problems (see 'Updates to this guide' section). There may be regulations on social distancing, group mixing, masks and other matters for some time so check the latest requirements in Italy before setting off. Communal accommodation in particular may be impacted – please take the required precautions to protect yourself and your fellow pilgrims.

ROUTE DESCRIPTIONS

Each stage is laid out in this format:

Route summary information
Information is included at the start of each stage that provides the specific starting and ending point as well as information summarizing the walk.

Total distance: Unless otherwise specified, the distance given is always based on the official route with all extraneous waypoints carefully edited out and the tracks smoothed to one waypoint for each 30m in distance. Expect the unedited tracks from your recreational GPS, smartphone app or step counter to be off by as much as 10–15% from distances based on the book's edited tracks.

Total ascent and descent: These figures record the up-and-down bumps that occur as you gain and lose elevation through the day. Elevation figures for GPS tracks in this book are provided through www.gpsvisualizer. com using the best of either ODP1, ASTER or NASA altitude data.

Difficulty: Using a formula that balances total distance, steepness and ascent/descent amounts, all stages are awarded one of four designations: 'Easy,' 'Moderate,' 'Moderately hard,' and 'Hard.'

Duration: No two pilgrims walk at exactly the same speed, so this book uses an algorithm that calculates duration based on 4 km/hr with an additional 5min added for every 100m of ascent, rounding the result to the nearest ¼ hour. Rest stops are not included in the duration total, so plan to add those to your schedule.

Percentage paved: This shows how much of the walk is on hard surfaces like concrete, tarmac, asphalt and cobblestones rather than softer surfaces like gravel, dirt roads and dirt paths.

Figure 1: Example of stage description and municipal information

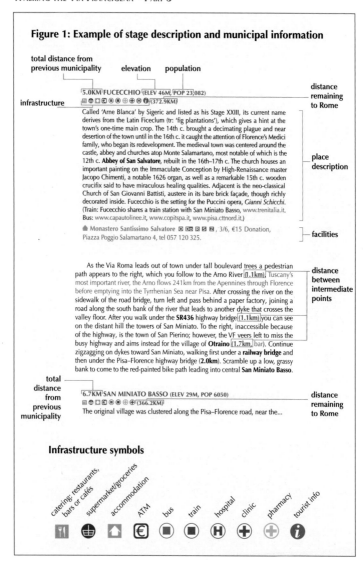

total distance from previous municipality

elevation

population

infrastructure

5.0KM FUCECCHIO (ELEV 46M, POP 23,082)

(372.9KM)

distance remaining to Rome

Called 'Arne Blanca' by Sigeric and listed as his Stage XXIII, its current name derives from the Latin Ficeclum (tr: 'fig plantations'), which gives a hint at the town's one-time main crop. The 14th c. brought a decimating plague and near desertion of the town until in the 16th c. it caught the attention of Florence's Medici family, who began its redevelopment. The medieval town was centered around the castle, abbey and churches atop Monte Salamartano, most notable of which is the 12th c. **Abbey of San Salvatore**, rebuilt in the 16th–17th c. The church houses an important painting on the Immaculate Conception by High-Renaissance master Jacopo Chimenti, a notable 1626 organ, as well as a remarkable 15th c. wooden crucifix said to have miraculous healing qualities. Adjacent is the neo-classical Church of San Giovanni Battisti, austere in its bare brick façade, though richly decorated inside. Fucecchio is the setting for the Puccini opera, *Gianni Schicchi*. (Train: Fucecchio shares a train station with San Miniato Basso, www.trenitalia.it. Bus: www.capautolinee.it, www.copitspa.it, www.pisa.cttnord.it.)

place description

🏠 Monastero Santissimo Salvatore ⊡ ⊞ 🅱 🆂 🆉 , 3/6, €15 Donation, Piazza Poggio Salamartano 4, tel 057 120 325.

facilities

As the Via Roma leads out of town under tall boulevard trees a pedestrian path appears to the right, which you follow to the Arno River (1.1km). Tuscany's most important river, the Arno flows 241km from the Apennines through Florence before emptying into the Tyrrhenian Sea near Pisa. After crossing the river on the sidewalk of the road bridge, turn left and pass behind a paper factory, joining a road along the south bank of the river that leads to another dyke that crosses the valley floor. After you walk under the **SR436** highway bridge (1.1km) you can see on the distant hill the towers of San Miniato. To the right, inaccessible because of the highway, is the town of San Pierino; however, the VF veers left to miss the busy highway and aims instead for the village of **Otraino** (1.7km, bar). Continue zigzagging on dykes toward San Miniato, walking first under a **railway bridge** and then under the Pisa–Florence highway bridge (**2.0km**). Scramble up a low, grassy bank to come to the red-painted bike path leading into central **San Miniato Basso**.

distance between intermediate points

total distance from previous municipality

6.7KM SAN MINIATO BASSO (ELEV 29M, POP 6050)

(366.2KM)

The original village was clustered along the Pisa–Florence road, near the...

distance remaining to Rome

Infrastructure symbols

catering: restaurants, bars or cafés

supermarket/groceries

accommodation

ATM

bus

train

hospital

clinic

pharmacy

tourist info

🍴   ⊕   🏠   €   ⊡   ⊡   Ⓗ   ✚   ✚   𝒊

Hostels: Distances from the start of the stage to all hostels are included in order to help you plan your stages.

Overview: This paragraph summarizes the stage and shares any special tips, recommendations or warnings walkers should know before beginning the walk.

Walking directions, distances and municipality information headings

Since the Via Francigena between Lucca and Rome is well marked, only moderately detailed walking descriptions are given for each stage. Bold type is used when a landmark is also labelled on the map, and intermediate distances are provided in the text between municipalities. Because underlying distance calculations are based on 100ths of a kilometer while intermediate distances are shown at 10ths of a kilometer some minor decimal rounding discrepancies naturally result when intermediate distances are added together. Municipalities with pilgrim lodgings have their own headings with 10 icons that indicate available services. Figure 1 shows the meaning of the various symbols and codes.

Accommodation listings

The EAVF has done an excellent job of creating a network of pilgrim-specific hostels located in churches, monasteries, convents, municipal facilities and church retreat houses that are not included in typical tourist resources like Booking.com. In collaboration

Symbol of the Confraternity of Pilgrims to Rome

with the EAVF and the Confraternity of Pilgrims to Rome (www.pilgrimstorome.org.uk) the names, contact information, cost and symbols of these and other low-cost lodgings are provided. Each has 10 important infrastructure elements to help you make your choice (see Figure 2 for the meaning of symbols).

Elevation profiles

Helpful elevation profiles are included so you see a graphical representation of distances and topography in each stage.

Maps

The maps in this guidebook are 'north up' and show the entire stage route at a scale of 1:100,000. Four cities – Lucca, Siena, Rome and Viterbo – are shown at a scale of around 1:25,000. The route is depicted by a solid red line, with optional route lines in dashed red and variant stages in solid blue. See the map key at the start of the book for more details about map symbols.

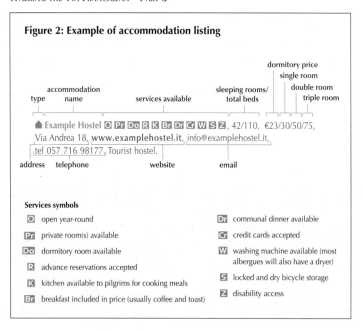

Figure 2: Example of accommodation listing

Services symbols

O	open year-round	Dr	communal dinner available
Pr	private room(s) available	Cr	credit cards accepted
Do	dormitory room available	W	washing machine available (most albergues will also have a dryer)
R	advance reservations accepted	S	locked and dry bicycle storage
K	kitchen available to pilgrims for cooking meals	Z	disability access
Br	breakfast included in price (usually coffee and toast)		

GPX AND ACCOMMODATION DOWNLOADS

A printout of the accommodation listings can be downloaded from www.cicerone.co.uk/1079. Always remember to visit the book's Cicerone website to find the latest book updates.

GPX tracks for the routes in this guidebook are available to download free at www.cicerone.co.uk/1079/GPX. GPX files are provided in good faith, but neither the author nor the publisher accept responsibility for their accuracy.

SECTION 1: TUSCANY

Pilgrims and tourists mix on the pedestrian main streets of central Siena

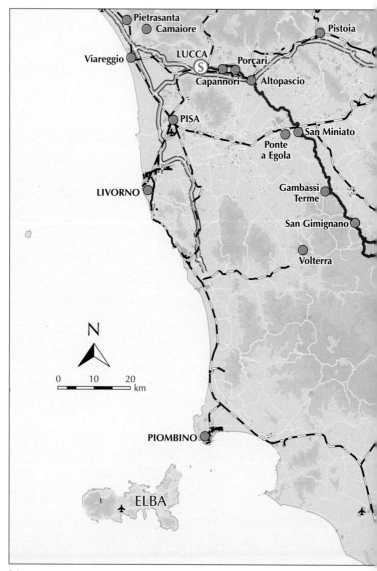

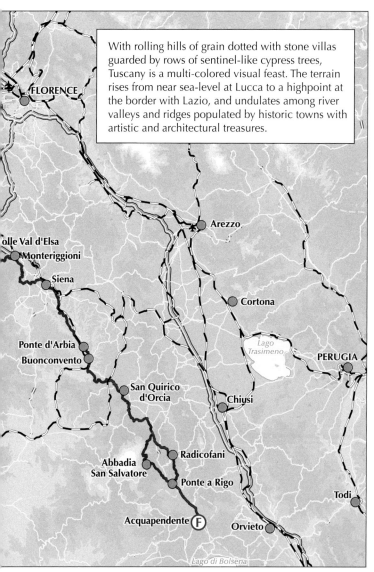

With rolling hills of grain dotted with stone villas guarded by rows of sentinel-like cypress trees, Tuscany is a multi-colored visual feast. The terrain rises from near sea-level at Lucca to a highpoint at the border with Lazio, and undulates among river valleys and ridges populated by historic towns with artistic and architectural treasures.

35

STAGE 1
Lucca to Altopascio

Start	Lucca, Piazza San Michele
Finish	Altopascio, Piazza dei Ospitalieri
Distance	18.3km
Total ascent	185m
Total descent	189m
Difficulty	Easy
Duration	4¾hr
Percentage paved	97%
Hostels	Capannori 6.6km, Badia Pozzeveri 16.4km, Altopascio 18.3km

This jaunt through the 'Plain of Lucca' is a stage of roadside walking, often accompanied by the noise of trucks and speeding cars. Some pilgrims instead spend 15 guilt-free minutes on the train and skip directly to Altopascio (twice-hourly departures from 05:00–22:00, €2.60, www.trenitalia.com). Those who walk will find a virtually flat landscape of suburbs, exurbs, commercial and industrial zones with intermediate refreshment stops at the towns of Cappanori and Porcari.

0.0KM LUCCA (ELEV 24M, POP 89,346)
🏨 ⊕ 🛏 🄲 ⊚ ⊕ ⊕ ⊕ 🄷 🄸 (410.5KM)

This red-roofed, sepia-tinted Tuscan town is best known for its fully-intact Renaissance-era city walls whose top surface – the **Via delle Mura Urbane** – makes for a convenient and scenic circumnavigation of the city on foot or by bike. Because of its historical sites, museums and innate charm, Lucca is an excellent place to spend an extra day or two for rest and exploration.

On a fertile plain at a narrow point among the low foothills of the Apuan Alps, this Tuscan gem traces its roots to the 3rd c. BC when coastal tribes created a settlement in what was then marsh land (*luk* is the Ligurian word for 'marsh'). The Romans found its location to be strategic and laid out a city along a typical

Roman template of perpendicular main streets culminating in four major city gates. Remnants of the Roman-era amphitheater remain at the **Piazza Anfiteatro,** and the Roman Forum, or central plaza, is preserved adjacent to the 11th–13th c. church of **San Michele in Foro**, right on the Via Francigena route. Here in Lucca, Julius Caesar, Pompey and Crassus affirmed their First Triumvirate alliance in the Lucca Conference of 56BC. As with most other central Italian cities after the fall of Rome, Lucca was ruled by a succession of northern European kingdoms. In 1160 it began a long period of uninterrupted independence, until in 1805 it was conquered by Napoleon, who installed his sister, Elisa, as its ruler. It later became part of the Duchy of Tuscany and was subsumed into a unified Italy in 1861.

Lucca hosts several important architectural and ecclesiastical monuments. The 11th–14th c. **Duomo of San Martino** hosts one of Italy's most important relics, the Volto Santa ('Sacred Countenance'), a carved wooden crucifix brought to Lucca in 782 and said to have been made by Nicodemus of the New Testament. On a column in the cathedral's façade is a small, carved labyrinth, along the same design as, but perhaps even older than, the famed labyrinth at Chartres. The 12th c. Romanesque **Basilica of San Frediano**, named after the 6th c. Irish saint who became bishop of Lucca, includes a monumental 13th c. mosaic on its façade. Inside, of special interest to VF pilgrims, is the tomb of St Richard the Pilgrim, likely a nobleman of Wessex, England, who died in Lucca in 722 during his pilgrimage to Rome and Jerusalem. Finally, the **Puccini Museum** remembers Lucca's favorite son and famed opera composer, Giacomo Puccini (1858–1924), at his birth home (€7, Corte San Lorenzo 9, www.puccinimuseum.it).

⌂ Casa del Pellegrino San Nicolao ◍ ◲ 🆁 🆂 4/10, €Donation, Via San Nicolao 76, tel 331 131 1522. A house of the Canonici Regolari Lateranensi hosted by Donatella and Stefano.

⌂ Misericordia ◍ ◲ 🆁 🅺 🆂 1/3, €Donation, Via Cesare Battisti 2, **www.misericordialucca.org**, tel 058 349 4902. Tel reservations only, from 09:00–18:00. Closed Sun.

⌂ Pellegrinario San Davino ◍ ◲ 🆁 🆂 🆉 1/10, €Donation, Via S Leonardo 12, **www.luccatranoi.it**, tel 058 353 576.

Follow along the south side of the San Michele in Foro church and continue through town on the Via Roma/Via Santa Croce, passing among shops and eateries, through the medieval Porta San Gervasio, and then the Renaissance **Porta Elisa**. Once outside Lucca's walls, cross into modern Lucca alongside the roundabout and onto the sidewalk of the SR439 for two blocks. Jog one block left onto the **Via Roma** and follow it to a small **shrine** (**2.9km**), where you fork to the right

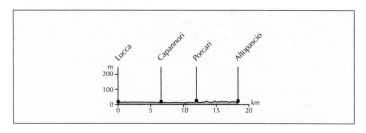

Lucca

🏛	Basilica di San Frediano	🏠	Pellegrinario San Davino
🏛	San Francesco	🏠	L'Arcicofraternita di Misericordia
🏛	San Michele in Foro	🏠	Casa del Pellegrino San Nicolao
🏛	Duomo di San Martino	●	Puccini Museum

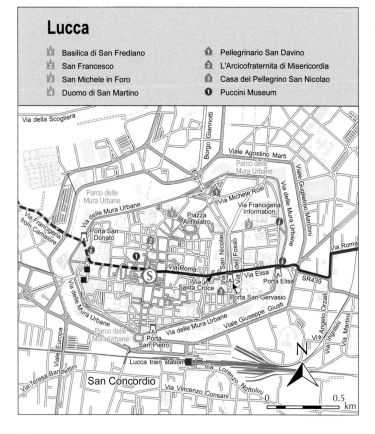

onto a blessedly quieter and smaller road heading in the same direction. Soon join a bike path alongside this road, passing the Church of **San Michele Arcangelo** (**1.6km**) on the left in the suburb of Antracolli. Much of the church's 12th c. construction can still be seen today, including remains of the original entrance. The tower dates from 1797. Cross two highways soon, leave the bike trail, pass a **cemetery** on your right, and make two left turns to come to central **Capannori**.

6.6KM CAPANNORI (ELEV 16M, POP 46,542)
🍴 🏠 🅒 ◉ ⊕ ⊕ (403.9KM)

Centerpiece of the town is its **Church of Saints Quirico and Giulitta**, whose 12th c. façade is in the Pisan style. Otherwise the town itself is relatively undistinguished, though just 2km outside is the Santuario della Madonnina, a 20th c. church connected to a 16th c. edifice that contains behind the altar an image of the Madonna del Carmine, believed to be responsible for miracles and wonders. (Bus: to Altopascio, www.lucca.cttnord.it.)

⌂ Ostello la Salana 🅞 🄿🅣 🄳🅞 🅁 🅚 🄱🅡 🄶🅕 🅦 🅢 🅩 5/24, €15/15/30/45, Via del Popolo 182, info@ostellolasalana.it, tel 058 341 4292 or 339 723 7912, bar & restaurant onsite, menu from €10. In winter book early.

Architectural influences of Pisa can be seen in the 12th c. façade of the church of San Quirico in Capannori

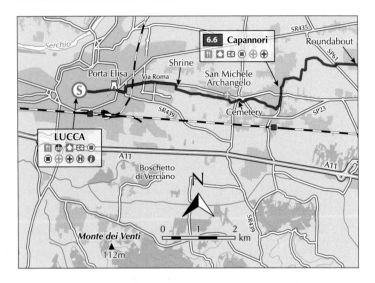

After the commercial district, join a pink-paved bike track that picks up to the right and zigzag your way through the outskirts of town, ultimately finding yourself on a quiet asphalt road among small cornfields. Cross the **SP-61** highway and walk on the narrow margin of an industrial road among small factories and warehouses where car and truck drivers give little thought to foot traffic. After passing alongside a **roundabout** (**3.2km**), the industrial traffic fades. Pass a few more small factories, cross a canal, turn right and soon the signs lead you into the heart of **Porcari**.

5.3KM PORCARI (ELEV 18M, POP 8604) 🏨 ⊕ 🏠 ⓒ ◉ ⊕ (398.6KM)

The town's first documented mention was in Lombard correspondence in 780. Over the centuries it became an important stopover on the Via Francigena, which Sigeric included as his Stage XXV Forcri. The hill behind town was a strategic lookout, used to guard the Plain of Lucca on Lucca's eastern flank and now site of the white marble 15th c. **Church of San Giusto**. In the Middle Ages the town's once-prominent castle was site of several battles, including the Battle of Altopascio on 23 September 1325 between Florence and the victorious forces of Lucca. Only a few traces of the castle remain today. (Bus: to Altopascio, www.lucca.cttnord.it.) Tourist lodging available.

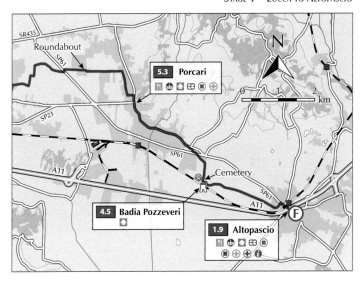

Continue along the Via Roma, forking right onto Via Roma Est as you leave town. Follow the pink sidewalk until it ends at the town's far boundary where you very soon fork right onto the first unpaved road of the day. Continue until it turns to asphalt in a few hundred meters and carefully cross the SP61 highway (**2.5km**), skirting behind a big-box pharmacy warehouse-store. Soon turn right between fields at a derelict house, briefly entering woods in the stage's only sylvan respite. A rest area and drinking fountain appear just before a **cemetery** and the large, archeological site of the Church of San Pietro and Abbey of **Badia Pozzeveri** with the modern hostel adjoining (**0.9km**).

4.5KM BADIA POZZEVERI (ELEV 20M, POP 2500) 🏠 (394.2KM)

From the 11th to 19th centuries a large monastery stood at this site, with the existing church and tower all that remain. The discovery of an adjacent, undisturbed, 1000-year-old cemetery has made it an important bio-archeological research site. Summer digs here under the guidance of the University of Pisa welcome archeological students from around the world. The town itself is a suburb with no services and is 1km beyond the archeological site and hostel.

Each summer archeologists return to Badia Pozzeveri to learn from human remains in the cemeteries surrounding the once prosperous abbey

🏠 Hostal Badia Ⓞ Pr Do R Br Dr Cr W S Z 6/23, €10/10/20/30, Via della Chiesa 1, info@iniziativaturistica.org, tel 335 702 5335 or 058 3180 8194. Dinner available for €10.

Pass the church on its left side and find a sidewalk paved in pink cobblestones beyond, which you follow through the sparse settlement of Badia Pozzeveri (**1.0km**, bakery). Turn right at the SP61 stop sign and cross the railroad tracks and then a bridge under the highway continuing to the tall brick tower and stucco façade of the Church of Sts. Jacopo, Cristoforo and Eligio in **Altopascio**.

1.9KM ALTOPASCIO (ELEV 20M, POP 9413)
🏨 ⊕ 🛏 🎒 ⊚ ⊛ ⊕ ⊕ 𝒊 (392.2KM)

Few towns along the Via Francigena connect as strongly to the Via Francigena as Altopascio. In the center of town remnants of its prominent medieval **pilgrim hospital** are preserved in the 51m bell tower, built in 1280, and in the façade, cloister, and apse of the Church of Sts. Jacopo, Cristoforo and Eligio, better known as **San Jacopo Maggiore** (St James the Great). Here in the 1070s, Matilda of Tuscany, one of medieval Europe's foremost female military and political leaders, founded the international Order of St James of Altopascio or 'Cavalieri del Tau.' This influential semi-military order spread its mission of hospitality and protection of pilgrims from here as far away as Portugal and Germany, and continued as an influential social, political and military force until it was suppressed and absorbed into the Order of St Lazarus in 1672. At the Calderone festival each year on St James Day, 25 July, a large cauldron of soup is paraded through town, commemorating the giant crock of potage from which pilgrims were fed here for centuries. Still ringing from the church tower is the 14th c. bell, La Smarrita (tr: 'The Lost One'), that summoned pilgrims and others each evening to safety inside the city walls.

The older and more charming part of the town lies behind the church tower, where three courtyards stand that roughly comprise the outline of the original castle and pilgrim hospital. To the left is the **Piazza dei Ospitalieri** with its interesting octagonal well, at the center is **Piazza Garibaldi** with the modern Magione dei Cavalieri pilgrim hostel, and to the right is **Piazza Ricasoli**, site of the La Magione del Tau restaurant that specializes in authentic medieval dishes and where the medieval city gate opens north at the end of Via San Jacopo. The most common family name in Altopascio is Pelligrini (tr: 'Pilgrims'). (Train: 2hr to San Miniato–Fucecchio, €10, www.trenitalia.com. Bus: 2hr incl transfer to San Miniato, www.capautolinee.it.)

⌂ Magione Cavalieri del Tau Ⓞ Ⓓ Ⓡ Ⓦ Ⓢ Ⓩ 2/10, €Donation, Piazza Ospitalieri 6, turismo@comune.altopascio.lu.it, tel 058 321 6280. Check-in by 18:00 at Biblioteca Comunale in Piazza Vittorio Emanuele. Closed Sun.

The La Smarrita bell in Altopascio's tower peals each evening before dark

STAGE 2
Altopascio to San Miniato

Start	Altopascio, Piazza dei Ospitalieri
Finish	San Miniato, Piazza Mazzini
Distance	28.7km
Total ascent	537m
Total descent	410m
Difficulty	Moderate
Duration	7¾hr
Percentage paved	44%
Hostels	Galleno 7.7km, Ponte a Cappiano 14.3km, San Miniato Basso 26km, San Miniato 28.7km

This pleasant stage can be grouped into three segments: through the woods, on the canal dykes with Fucecchio in the middle, and up the final hill. Together they amount to a memorable and scenic day, much of it spent aiming at the distant Tower of Federico II at stage end. Intermediate stops at Galleno, Ponte a Cappiano, Fucecchio, Ontraino and San Miniato Basso offer refreshment. In good weather the sun can be an adversary due to lack of shade on the long canal walks.

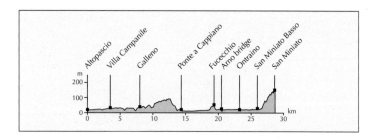

Return to the pink cobblestone sidewalk as you head out of town, at rush hour accompanied by the roar of traffic. Pass the **cemetery** with its large, domed building and turn right at a roundabout (**1.6km**, bakery), finding a quiet path through the woods after the turn. Arrive soon at **Villa Campanile** (**1.9km**, bar),

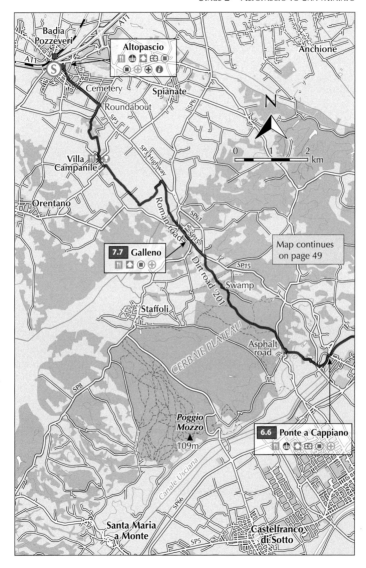

a tiny village with a namesake belltower. After town a gravel track leads to the left through small fields first and then quiet woods. Cross a small bridge over a seasonal stream in the forest and begin a couple of moderate climbs before the path ends at a gravel road and you turn very briefly onto the busy **SP3** highway (**2.9km**). Very soon fork right onto a gravel road that before long is paved in rounded cobblestones. The ancient Via Francigena route here coincides with this antique roadway, once called the Via Francesca. Look for the milestone 'No. 13' of the original route. The old track ends at an asphalt road leading into **Galleno**.

7.7KM GALLENO (ELEV 37M, POP 609) ⏸ 🏠 ◉ ⊕ (384.5KM)

The town grew around the Via Francigena and is mentioned in records as early as the 11th c. It exists today as a pleasant, modern village centered along the SP15 highway, with few traces of its medieval past. (Bus: routes 240, 290, 291, www.pisa.cttnord.it.)

🏠 **Casetta dei Pellegrini** ◉ 🛏 🇰 🇸 2/5, €Donation, Via della Chiesa 20, san-pietrogalleno@gmail.com, tel 057 129 9931 or 366 999 7072. At the Church of San Pietro.

Follow alongside the **SP15** highway out of town until the track branches off to the right after the SP15 joins the SP61 (1.2km). Here a **dirt road** marked '201' leads into the quiet and wooded **Cerbaie Plateau**, a low rise of 120sq km that separates the Provinces of Pisa and Florence and here is sparsely filled with scrubby pine trees. The sometimes muddy and rutted dirt road ascends, often steeply, and you pass a large swamp on the left. After the better part of an hour the path joins a busy asphalt road (**3.3km**), which you follow on a pathway on the left side. Soon you see views of towns in the valley below, and in about 600m you switch back to the left and follow a trail downhill that before long turns into an asphalt driveway leading down into the town of **Ponte a Cappiano**.

6.6KM PONTE A CAPPIANO (ELEV 19M, POP 1200)
⏸ ⊕ 🏠 🇨 ◉ ⊕ (377.9KM)

Identified as Sigeric's Stage XXIV Aqua Nigra (tr: 'Black Water'), the town perhaps earned its medieval name from the brackish waters of the Usciana Canal over which its bridge sits. The span itself was of strategic importance in medieval wars between Lucca and Florence, who each fortified or destroyed it at various times

The four arches of the 16th c. Medici bridge span the Usiana Canal at Ponte a Cappiano

in its history. At its high point it included three drawbridges, a system of locks to hold back the waters of the canal, and various mills and forges. In the 16th c. Cosimo di Medici of Florence rebuilt it into its present form, earning it the name 'the Medici Bridge.' For centuries the Hospitallers of Altopascio safeguarded the bridge for the sake of its Via Francigena pilgrim traffic, and today it houses a pilgrim hostel. (Bus: #20, www.capautolinee.it.)

⌂ Ostello il Ponte dei Medici ⦿ ℙᵗ ᴰᵒ ℝ 𝕂 ℂᶠ 𝕎 ⓢ ℤ 4/15, €20/-/-/-, Viale Cristoforo Colombo 237, ostellopontedeimedici@gmail.com, tel 057 129 7831.

Partway across the bridge turn left and descend onto the pathway atop the righthand dyke of the canal. Before long turn right onto another dyke, cross a footbridge and a few roads. The dyke walls turn to concrete at the entrance to the flat, lower residential suburbs of Fucecchio. Cross the **SP11** roadway, then the Viale Bonaparte and turn right onto **Via Sant'Antonio (4.4km)** to begin a flight of 72 steps to reach the upper, older city. The signs lead you through Piazza Garibaldi and Piazza Veneto, then up the steps to the churches of San Giovanni Battista and San Salvatore, behind which is a lookout from the town's highest point at Poggio Salamartano, which offers wide vistas over the Lower Arno Valley and Cerbaie Plateau. Follow signs downhill through Piazza Cavour to find the cafés and shops of modern **Piazza Montanelli**.

5.0KM FUCECCHIO (ELEV 46M, POP 23,082)
🚇 🚻 🏧 🅲 🅿 🅾 ⊕ ⊕ 🅗 🅘 (372.9KM)

Called 'Arne Blanca' by Sigeric and listed as his Stage XXIII, its current name derives from the Latin Ficeclum (tr: 'fig plantations'), which gives a hint at the town's one-time main crop. The 14th c. brought a decimating plague and near desertion of the town until in the 16th c. it caught the attention of Florence's Medici family, who began its redevelopment. The medieval town was centered around the castle, abbey and churches atop Monte Salamartano, most notable of which is the 12th c. **Abbey of San Salvatore**, rebuilt in the 16th–17th c. The church houses an important painting on the Immaculate Conception by High-Renaissance master Jacopo Chimenti, a notable 1626 organ, as well as a remarkable 15th c. wooden crucifix said to have miraculous healing qualities. Adjacent is the neo-classical Church of San Giovanni Battisti, austere in its bare brick façade, though richly decorated inside. Fucecchio is the setting for the Puccini opera, *Gianni Schicchi*. (Train: Fucecchio shares a train station with San Miniato Basso, www.trenitalia.it. Bus: www.capautolinee.it, www.copitspa.it, www.pisa.cttnord.it.)

🏠 Monastero Santissimo Salvatore 🅾 🅳🅾 🆁 🆂 🆉 3/6, €15 Donation, Piazza Poggio Salamartano 4, tel 057 120 325.

As the Via Roma leads out of town under tall boulevard trees a pedestrian path appears to the right, which you follow to the Arno River (**1.1km**). Tuscany's most important river, the Arno flows 241km from the Apennines through Florence before emptying into the Tyrrhenian Sea near Pisa. After crossing the river on the sidewalk of the road bridge, turn left and pass behind a paper factory, joining a road along the south bank of the river that leads to another dyke that crosses the valley floor. After you walk under the **SR436** highway bridge (**1.1km**) you can see on the distant hill the towers of San Miniato. To the right, inaccessible because of the highway, is the town of San Pierino; however, the VF veers left to miss the busy highway and aims instead for the village of **Otraino** (**1.7km**, bar). Continue zigzagging on dykes toward San Miniato, walking first under a **railway bridge** and then under the Pisa–Florence highway bridge (**2.0km**). Scramble up a low, grassy bank to come to the red-painted bike path leading into central **San Miniato Basso**.

6.7KM SAN MINIATO BASSO (ELEV 29M, POP 6050)
🚇 🚻 🏧 🅲 🅿 🅾 ⊕ ⊕ (366.2KM)

The original village was clustered along the Pisa–Florence road, near the bridge over the Rio Pidocchio. From this the village name was corrupted to 'Pinocchio,' which was changed in 1924 to San Miniato Basso. (Train: on the Pisa–Florence line. Bus: multiple lines, www.pisa.cttnord.it.)

⌂ **Misericordia** Ⓞ ⒟ⓞ Ⓡ Ⓢ Ⓩ 1/6, €Donation, Piazza Vincenzo Cuoco 9, misericordiasmb@libero.it, tel 057 141 9455 or 339 872 3682.

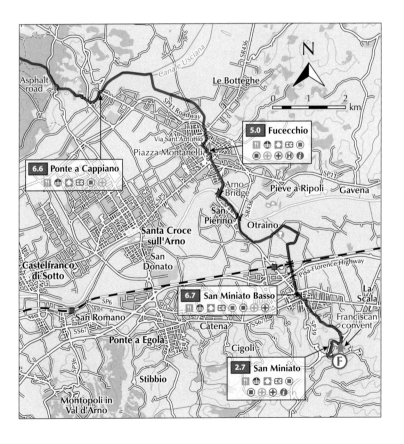

A grassy canal-side path leads from San Miniato Basso to the towers of San Miniato above

The signs now direct you through the center of town and onto a narrow path atop another dyke, where you look down onto the gardens of suburban homes until the canal walk ends and you join a steep asphalt road leading up to the hilltop. Follow the road and then a gravel pathway before a final steep climb on asphalt. If you are staying at the **Franciscan convent**, fork left (**1.8km**, dir. Calenzano) when you see its hulking brick form and low, yellow tower on the hill just above. Otherwise, fork right to the center of **San Miniato** on the far side of the hill (**0.9km**).

2.7KM SAN MINIATO (ELEV 147M, POP 27,585)
🏨 ⊕ 🏠 🄲 ⊙ ⊚ ⊕ ⊕ 🛈 (363.5KM)

Named after a 3rd c. Florentine martyr, the Y-shaped hilltop town of San Miniato sits at the strategic intersection of the ancient Lucca–Siena and Florence–Pisa roads. Its three 100m hills made it a prized fortress of the Lombards, who built a castle here in the 11th c., when it briefly surpassed Florence in importance as the Tuscan capital for the Lombard Holy Roman Empire. In the 12th c. Emperor Frederick II expanded the fortress and built its emblematic landmark, the tall **'Federico II' tower**, which was rebuilt in 1958 after being destroyed by the Nazis in WWII. Much of the town's medieval character remains in its many prized *palazzi*, as well as in the ecclesiastical buildings at the summit campus that include the **Duomo of Sant'Assunta**, its asymmetrical San Matilde clock tower that was originally part of the medieval fortress, the Diocesan Museum, which features works of several celebrated Renaissance masters, the 18th c. Sanctuary of the Holy Crucifix, which splendidly houses an 11th c. cross, and the **Church and Convent of San Francesco**, who is said to have founded the two in his visit in 1211. (Train: station shared with San Miniato Basso. Bus: #320, www.pisa.cttnord.it.)

🏠 Convento San Francesco Ⓞ P̲r̲ R̲ B̲r̲ D̲r̲ W̲ S̲ 25/70, €10/-/-/-, Piazza San Francesco 1, sanminiato@nuoviorizzonti.org, tel 057 143 051, €25 half-board; Oct–Apr extra €5 per person. Mon–Fri 19:00 Mass, Sun 09:00.

🏠 Ostello San Miniato Ⓞ D̲o̲ R̲ K̲ W̲ S̲ Z̲ 3/13, €17/-/-/-, Via Vittime del Duomo 4, ostellosanminiato@gmail.com, tel 338 799 7004.

🏠 Affittacamere San Miniato Ⓞ P̲r̲ D̲o̲ R̲ S̲ Z̲ 6/11, €19/30/40/-, Via Giosuè Carducci 2, **www.affittacameresanminiato.it**, affittacameresanminiato@gmail. com, tel 353 389 0839.

The dome of the 18th c. Sanctuary of the Holy Crucifix towers over an 11th c. cross believed to inspire miracles

STAGE 3
San Miniato to Gambassi Terme

Start	San Miniato, Piazza Mazzini
Finish	Gambassi Terme, Piazza Roma
Distance	24.1km
Total ascent	820m
Total descent	639m
Difficulty	Moderately hard
Duration	7hr
Percentage paved	27%
Hostels	Chianni (Ostello Sigerico) 23.1km, Gambassi Terme 24.1km

Sandwiched between two sometimes-harrowing roadway walks is a very lovely ramble along paths in a sublime Tuscan countryside of hilly farmland and cypress trees. Though picturesque and pleasant in fair weather, the quiet stretch in the middle is devoid of services and sometimes of shade. On a sunny day bring sunscreen and, on any day, bring a lunch and plenty of water.

Leave San Miniato Alto downhill on Via de'Mangiadori, passing the Church of Santi Sebastiano e Rocco in Piazza Buonaparte and continuing among other vintage buildings. Turn right just before **Piazza XX Settembre** (**0.7km**, fountain), continuing downhill to join a highway. The highway ascends, reaching a summit just before a rest area across from a former **Capuchin convent** (**0.8km**). Follow along on the asphalt road among scattered farmhouses and olive groves to the hamlet of **Calenzano** (**0.9km**, bar), last eatery until near the end of the stage.

> Lying 2km directly north of Calenzano is the archeological site of **San Genesio**, Sigeric's Stage XXII and a thriving village until it was destroyed in 1248 by forces from San Miniato. A diminutive archeological museum there hosts findings from the 4th c. BC to AD1248.

Turn left soon afterward, watching for speeding cars on this dangerous stretch. A right at the San Miniato **swimming pool complex** (**1.1km**) takes you off the highway onto a quieter road that follows the ridge line among olive groves and

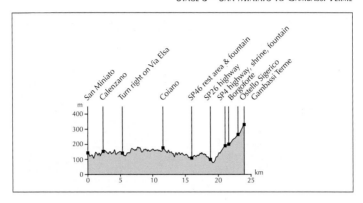

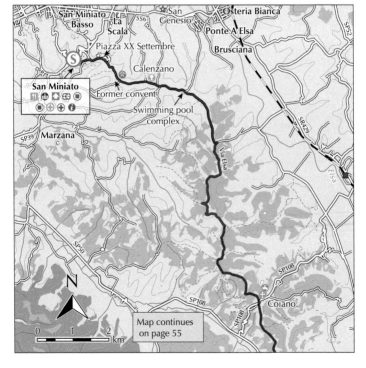

Map continues
on page 55

vineyards with occasionally views to each side. At a rest area with no water partway down the hill turn right onto **Via Elsa** (**1.9km**) and follow this dirt and gravel road, finally leaving the noisy cars behind.

Now begins the very long stretch in farmland, at first in and out among stands of trees and at one point with wide views back toward San Miniato. Pass several large farm homes, most complete with chickens, dogs and lazy cats, until you hear the sound of cars on the SP108 ahead, letting you know you are arriving at the hamlet of **Coiano** (**6.3km**, water).

A marker near the farmhouse of Campriano shows the distance to the water fountain at Coiano

The abandoned state of its proud 12th c. **Church of Santi Pietro e Paolo** signals that Coiano's days as a prominent town are behind it. Sigeric stopped here as his Stage XXI and in the 13th c. it was listed as one of 36 castles in the San Miniato district. The church's tower was completed in 1837 and the large, Romanesque church building was restored a century later. Coiano's most infamous son is anarchist Gaetano Bresci, who assassinated King Umberto I of Italy in 1900. Tuscan anarchists commissioned a monument to Bresci for Coiano but its installation here was blocked by the Italian government. On the far side of the tall church is a pilgrim rest area and water fountain.

The first transit of the Swiss Guard is remembered in a weathered plaque

Cross the **SP108**, passing the Castello Coiano Winery onto a dirt path that merges with a narrow dirt road continuing along the ridgeline in a gradual descent. Pass a derelict house on the left and begin descending, coming to a shaded bench with a plaque labeled with the years 1506–2006. A detachment of 150 Swiss soldiers rested here as they journeyed to Rome at the request of Pope Julius II, ultimately becoming first of a long line of Swiss Guards responsible for the Popes' security at the Vatican.

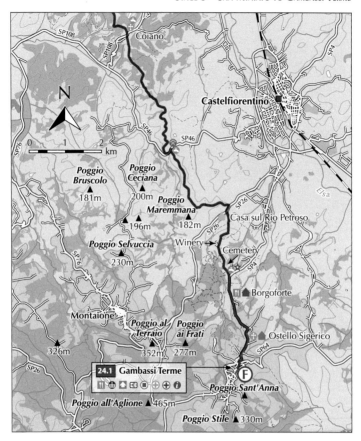

Come to a section of the dirt road that is cut into the hillside, pass a panorama over a small lake and rolling hills, and after a time finally come out of the forest to enter a zone of low, rolling hayfields that stretch far into the distance.

Descend to the **SP46** highway, crossing to a shaded rest area. Signs direct you 100m left along the highway to a water fountain (**4.4km**), where you switchback right to climb a gravel track up the hillside. Pass among farm buildings and olive groves then turn right at the **SP26** highway (**3.0km**), on which you walk briefly before crossing the highway toward **Casa sul Rio Petroso** *agriturismo*

(🏠 Casa sul Rio Petroso O Pr R K Br Dr Cr W S Z, 5/8, €25/25/50/75, Via San Michelino in piano 63, casariopetroso@yahoo.com, tel 347 210 8595, 349 529 1804. Reservation req.). After the *agriturismo* the long climb to Gambassi Terme begins. Pass a **winery** on the right, then a **cemetery** on the left, coming just before the **SP4** highway to a small shrine with a rest area and water fountain (**2.1km**, bus routes 33, 34, 80 to Gambassi Terme).

Forced back onto the road now, an occasional path to the right of the guard-rail offers a haven from speeding vehicles. Follow the SP4 to **Borgoforte** (**0.6km**, bar, restaurant, B&B see below) and its very welcome pilgrim bar/restaurant. Continue onward, passing **Ostello Sigerico**, a beloved pilgrim overnight, located at the Church of Santa Maria Assunta of Chianni (**1.4km**). Follow alongside the road up into **Gambassi Terme**, passing the pilgrim information office and coming to the modern Church of Cristo Re. Though the signs point you uphill into town, you can also turn left here to continue on to the next stage. Otherwise walk three blocks uphill to find the shops and bars of Piazza Roma (**1.0km**).

24.1KM GAMBASSI TERME (ELEV 327M, POP 4798)
🏨 🍴 🏧 🏦 ⊙ ⊕ ⊕ 🛈 (339.4KM)

Gambassi Terme, known for its wide views of Tuscan countryside and for its thermal baths, lies at the crossroads of the ancient Via Volterra and the Via Francigena. Though the town has been inhabited since Neolithic times, its most notable building is the 12th c. **Church of Santa Maria Assunta**, a few hundred meters below town at Chianni. The religious community there hosted pilgrims on the

Via Francigena, including Archbishop Sigeric, who identified it as his Stage XX. A hostel at the church complex carries his name and the restored edifice is a fine example of the local Romanesque style. While its interior is austere, its columnar capitals are richly sculpted and it preserves an antique pipe organ playable today.

The village of Gambassi Terme has few buildings as old as this, since much of the town was sacked and destroyed in medieval wars against nearby San Gimignano. Called only 'Gambassi' until 1977, its name was changed to highlight the presence of its **Terme Acqua di Pillo** (*terme* tr: 'hot springs', see www. termeviafrancigena.club). Adjacent to Piazza Roma is the town's clock tower, and opposite is the communal park, formerly the grounds of a large *palazzo*. The town's most famous citizen is **Giovanni Francesco Gonnelli**, a notable 17th c. sculptor, who in spite of being blind in later life continued his vocation as sculptor. His blindness was verified by passing a test where he was required to sculpt a work in total darkness. He also is said to have accurately sculpted a bust of his wife solely from memory.

🛏 **La Sosta di Roberto** (call for price and facilities), Loc. Borgoforte, Via Santa Maria Chianni 10A, lasostadiroberto@hotmail.com, tel 380 128 0722.

🛏 **Ostello Sigerico** Ⓞ Pr Do R Br Df Gr S Z 12/40, €12/-/34/-, Pieve Santa Maria in Chianni, ostello.sigerico@yahoo.com, tel 324 796 8837 or 057 163 9044. Kitchen available in winter or for large groups. Advisable to call for reservations in summer. Community dinner €10.

Limited additional tourist accommodation is available in Gambassi Terme.

A small chapel sits off the Piazza Roma at the heart of Gambassi Terme

STAGE 4
Gambassi Terme to San Gimignano

Start	Gambassi Terme, Piazza Roma
Finish	San Gimignano, Piazza del Duomo
Distance	13.7km
Total ascent	476m
Total descent	468m
Difficulty	Moderate
Duration	4hr
Percentage paved	48%
Hostels	San Gimignano 13.7km

This is the best of Tuscany – vineyards and wineries spread out over low, rolling hills outlined with tall cypress trees and olive groves as far as the eye can see. At stage end is one of Italy's best-preserved medieval towns, well known to tourists but still full of charm for pilgrims looking to experience the Tuscany of yesterday. Though the walk is short, an early start leaves more time for touring the treasures of historic San Gimignano. If you haven't reserved your ticket to the Duomo, you'll want to do that right away.

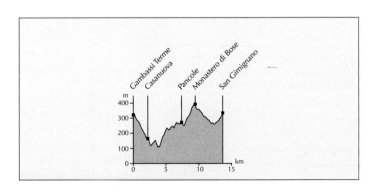

The tall towers of San Gimignano's skyline are visible from a great distance

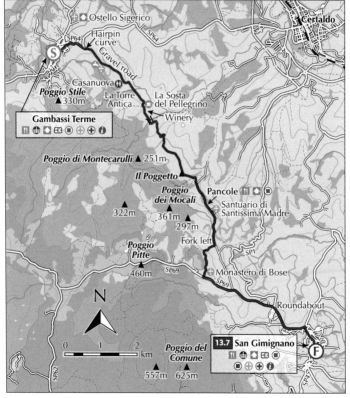

Ostello Sigerico

Certaldo

Hairpin curve

SP64

Gravel road

S

Casanuova

Poggio Stile
▲330m

La Torre
Antica

La Sosta
del Pellegrino

Winery

Gambassi Terme

Poggio di Montecarulli ▲ 251m

Il Poggetto

*Poggio
dei Mocali*

Pancole

Santuario di
Santissima Madre

▲
322m

361m ▲
297m

Fork left

SP1

*Poggio
Pitte*

SP69

▲
460m

Monastero di Bose

SP69

Roundabout

N

0   1   2
km

13.7 San Gimignano

F

*Poggio del
Comune*

▲   ▲
557m   625m

SPK2

SP2

The oddly placed signs in the city center would walk you in circles, so instead, from Piazza Roma head to Via Gonnelli alongside the clock tower, walking through the parking area at its end and veering left onto Via de Monache. Continue downhill and turn right onto the **SP64** highway where you soon find yourself pointing in the direction of San Gimignano, whose towers are visible on a clear day ahead in the distance. At a **hairpin curve** pick up a quiet asphalt road to the right and say goodbye for now to the highway.

A tiny, neo-classical chapel stands sentinel at a farm outside Gambassi Terme

The road quickly turns to gravel and descends through vine-covered trees, aiming again directly at San Gimignano, often visible ahead. Come to an elegant chapel in the neo-classical style (**1.5km**, fountain) beside tall cypress trees and fork left, heading downhill with vineyards on the left. Come to **Casanuova** (**0.7km**, WC), a pilgrim-friendly winery and olive farm. Continue to descend and at the bottom of the valley pass **La Torre Antica** Winery and rest stop (**0.5km**).

After crossing a seasonal stream, continue uphill to the pilgrim rest area **La Sosta del Pellegrino** (**0.5km**, café). Come to a summit, complete with **winery**, and look ahead to see confirmation the day will be spent crossing a succession of ridges. Descend now, and near the bottom of this valley cross a high brick **bridge** over a seasonal stream surprisingly far below. Soon begin your first major climb of the day on a heavily eroded road. If you look behind, Gambassi Terme is visible on a clear day. Come to a quiet asphalt road (**3.4km**) and turn right here, just before an *agriturismo* below. Before long arrive at the settlement of **Pancole** (**0.8km**, café at hotel, www.hotellerenaie.com).

The town's **Santuario di Maria Santissima Madre della Divina Provvidenza**, sight of a 17th c. apparition of the Virgin Mary, stands astride the highway. In a grotto below and to the right is a life-sized crèche scene, while the church above, decorated in warm tones, hosts a notable 15th c. fresco of a breast-feeding Virgin by Pier Francesco Fiorentino. The original church was destroyed by Nazis in WWII but was rebuilt in 1949. Skip the church and grotto by walking the road or turn right and descend on steps to see the life-sized characters of the Nativity and then the church above.

Continue alongside the asphalt road, climbing the hill on a gravel road to the right. Fork left (**1.1km**) to head up the hill more steeply, passing among buildings of a farm complex. As the road nears the highway beyond, the **Monastero di Bose** (**0.9km**, gift shop) stands to the left.

Three of San Gimignanos towers stand above Piazza delle Erbe

The **ecumenical monastery of Bose** was established in 1965 at Biella, near Ivrea, with both men and women in a community of prayer, celibacy, worship and sacramental life. Since 2013 a subset of Bose friars has worshiped here in the simple and elegant 13th c. Church of Santa Maria Assunta a Cellole.

Now the gravel road turns to asphalt and makes it way to the **SP69** highway, where you turn left to carefully walk along the road. At a **roundabout** (**2.5km**), cross to the right and begin the day's final ascent through the modern town and then into the medieval Porta San Matteo of **San Gimignano**. Continue along Via San Matteo to Piazza del Duomo at the heart of town (**1.7km**).

13.7KM SAN GIMIGNANO (ELEV 335M, POP 7780)
🏠 ⊕ 🛄 🅒 ◉ ◎ ⊕ ⊕ 🛈 (325.7KM)

Honored as a UNESCO world heritage site, the city center of San Gimignano is a jewel of medieval architecture. Most notable of its buildings are its 15 remaining medieval towers (there once were 72), erected by patrician families to safeguard their valuables and display their affluence. Other fine examples of Romanesque and Gothic architecture are the Palazzo Comunale, the Collegiate Church and the Church of Sant'Agostino, each of which contain frescoes dating to the 14th and 15th c. Pilgrims can easily miss the **Church of Sant'Agostino**, which is behind and to the left as you enter Porta San Matteo. The 13th c. building is dominated by priceless 15th c. frescoes around its altar. At the heart of town, the interior of the 12th c. **Duomo Collegiate Church** is a festival of black and white marble, festooned with stunning 14th c. frescoes on New and Old Testament themes. Local Saint Fina is also remembered in a frescoed chapel dedicated to her on the church's right side (€4, reservations recommended, www.duomosangimignano. it). Centerpiece of the nearby 13th c. **Palazzo Comunale** is the Maestà fresco, painted in 1317 by Lippo Memmi. The 14th c. **Torre Grossa**, tallest tower in town, offers a panoramic view at the top (€9 allows entry to tower and all town museums, www.sangimignanomusei.it/eng).

San Gimignano traces its roots to the 3rd c. BC, though records first mention it during the 1st c. BC when a Roman nobleman, Silvio, fled Rome and built a castle here. The town bore his name until the 5th c. when it was renamed to honor saintly Bishop Geminianus, who intervened to save the town from the armies of Atilla the Hun. In the Middle Ages it became an important stopping point along the Via Francigena and is listed by Sigeric as his Stage XIX. The town flourished until 1348, when the Black Plague killed half its population, which led to a decline in economic and political importance that – to our good fortune – saved it from redevelopment in later centuries. Since the 12th c. San Gimignano has been famous for its saffron and the town celebrates the spice in an annual festival in late October/early November.

🏠 **Convento Sant'Agostino** 🄳🄾 1/4, €Donation, Piazza San Agostino 10, tel 057 790 7012.

🏠 **A Spasso nel Tempo** 🄾 🄿🅃 🅁 🅂 2/7, €-/-/70/90, Via G. Matteotti 8, info@aspassoneltempo.net, tel 333 602 2748.

🏠 **Donna Nobile** 🄾 🄿🅃 🅁 🄲🄵 🅂 12/35, €57/82/102/112, Via delle Romite 15, **www.donnanobile.it**, info@donnanobile.it, tel 347 785 6352 or 366 345 5414. Low season reduced rates.

🏠 **Palazzo Buonaccorsi** 🄾 🄿🅃 🅁 🄲🄵 🅆 🅂 6/13, €-/30/60/-, Via San Matteo 95, info@palazzobuonaccorsi.it, tel 057 794 0908 or 349 807 9349. Breakfast and half-board available.

🔺 **Villaggio del Pellegrino – Camping Boschetto di Piemma** 🄾 🅁 🄱🄵 🄳🄵 🄲🄵 🅆, 95/154, €-/30/50/-, Via Santa Lucia 38/c., info@villaggiodelpellegrino.it, tel 057 790 7134. Tent camping allowed. Rooms in mobile homes available. Swimming pool.

STAGE 5

San Gimignano to Monteriggioni

Start	San Gimignano, Piazza del Duomo
Finish	Monteriggioni, Church of Santa Maria
Distance	27.4km (30.9km through Quartaia)
Total ascent	719m (753m through Quartaia)
Total descent	777m (812m through Quartaia)
Difficulty	Moderately hard
Duration	7¾hr
Percentage paved	19%
Hostels	Colle di Val d'Elsa 12.4km, Gracciano 15.8km, Abbadia d'Isola 23.7km, Monteriggioni 27.4km

The route penetrates deep into the forests, fields, olive orchards and vineyards of the Val d'Elsa culminating at a picturesque jewel of Tuscan medieval charm – the castle village of Monteriggioni. Walkers choose either the official route through Quartaia, which though quiet and green lacks services, or the recommended but more urban, shorter and better-served route through the scenic and historic town of Colle di Val d'Esla. Before starting out, make a stop at the shops and supermarket of San Gimignano, particularly if you have chosen the longer variant.

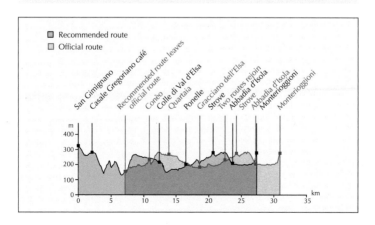

Walk along Via San Giovanni, descending through the historic center of town, and exit the walls through their far gate, Porta San Giovanni. A right and a left turn lead downhill onto the Strada Comunale di Santa Lucia, passing the buildings of the **Monastero di Monteoliveto** (now a villa) while enjoying views

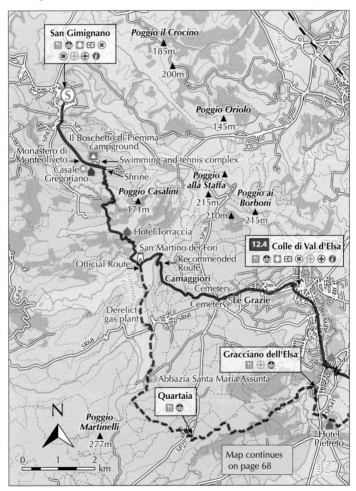

Map continues on page 68

64

back to San Gimignano. Pass **Casale Gregoriano** (**2.1km**, rooms, café, www. casalegregoriano.com/en), and then pass **Il Boschetto di Piemma campground**, followed by the town's **tennis and swimming pool** complex on your left. Soon turn right at a small shrine onto a gravel road and begin to descend quickly. Ahead you can see that the terrain consists of a series of ridges and valleys, none too tall or deep, that will constitute the bulk of the upcoming walk.

Continue now among vineyards and small forests on sometimes rutted roads. After crossing a seasonal creek, walk uphill toward the front gate of the **Hotel Torraccia di Chiusi** (**3.7km**, www.torracciadichiusi.it) and then continue downhill through forest, walking between buildings of the Aiano farm. Continue to descend, coming to the lowest point of the stage at **Torrente Foci** (**0.9km**) that is crossable on broad, flat white stones. Scholars identify the valley of this stream as the likely location for Sigeric's stage XVIII, labeled Sce Martin in Fosse. While the relic of a mill stands nearby, nothing remains of what is believed to have been the medieval monastery that hosted the archbishop. In about 400m see signs for the main and optional routes.

Recommended option through Colle di Val d'Elsa (11.9km)
Turn left at the option and climb at a moderately steep grade in the forest. Come out of the forest into olive orchards, where the track turns to asphalt and a sign announces you have arrived at the outskirts of the hamlet of **Camaggiori**. Continue through olive groves and enjoy the road's flat meander in countryside atop a wide plateau. Pass a grand **cemetery** on the right, and on the left its 1960's-era cousin. Continue on toward the **SR68** highway, turning left once you reach it, and walking on its spacious right-hand side. Continue toward the historic center of **Colle di Val d'Elsa** on a sidewalk of concrete pavers, either following signs to walk left of the stout, medieval battlements, or simply walking through the Porta Nuova among some of the 16th and 17th c. *palazzi* and charming cafés and bars that line the single street atop the narrow ridge. Continue to reach the historic center's castle by crossing a bridge and passing through a gate beneath the Palazzo Campana.

12.4KM COLLE DI VAL D'ELSA (ELEV 203M, POP 21,600)
🔢 ⊕ 🏧 🄴 ⊙ ⊕ ⊕ **❶** (313.3KM)

Modern Colle di Val d'Elsa (tr: 'hill of the Elsa Valley') is recognized internationally for its fine lead crystal glassware, producing 15% of the world's supply. The town traces its roots to the 4th c. BC, though it is first mentioned in 9th c. documents. Here a 1269 battle, remembered in Dante's *Divine Comedy* (Purgatorio, Canto XIII), saw a vastly outnumbered Guelph army, supporting the Pope, overcome

View from the castle in Colle di Val d'Elsa

the town's castle held by the numerically superior Ghibellines, supporters of the Holy Roman Empire. The old town is laid out in the shape of a sideways capital 'T' and you enter at the Porta Nuova at the bottom of the stem, walking up the stem to the **Castello** at the stem's top. There you turn right to one arm of the 'T', heading downhill to the lower town. In this sequence, just after entering the Porta Nuova come to the **Museo San Pietro**, featuring local religious art from the 6th– 20th c. while further on is the related Archeological Museum (see info for both at www.collealtamusei.it) in the 14th c. **Palazzo Pretorio**. Continuing to the oldest, castello part of town, pass many 15th and 16th c. palaces of noble families, as well as the squarish, neo-classical 17th c. **Co-cathedral of Saints Marcial and Alberto**. Continue on to the dramatic viewpoint at the end of the old city. From here a series of steps (or a convenient elevator) lead to the lower part of town, which features the Crystal Museum (€4, www.museodelcristallo.it).

🏠 **Convento di San Francesco** 🅿️ 🄳ₒ 🆁 🆂 20/50, €10/-/-/-, Via San Francesco 4, tabor@arcidiocesi.siena.it, tel 057 792 0040 or 327 679 9124. Groups only in winter. Best to call 1–2 days before arrival.

🏠 **Parrocchia di San Marziale** 🄾 🄳ₒ 🆁 🄺 1/8, €Donation, Loc. San Marziale #1, feaesi@gmail.com, tel 329 746 5518.

Continue on until a switchback ramp leads downhill to the city's lower, newer neighborhoods. Watch for the pedestrian signal to cross through the narrow gate of the lower city and continue onward, forking left onto the Via Maremanna Vecchia at a jumble of intersections that is the main, lower piazza. This diversion takes you briefly off the busy, main road, but you return to it in short order and join the **Viale dei Mille** arterial full of apartment homes and car dealerships. After nearly 2km on this noisy road, cross the Elsa River (**3.4km**) on a high, pedestrian bridge and turn left (the parish church on the left hosts the **San Marziale** pilgrim hostel). This road leads you under the **SP541** highway and around a low hill, passing through the village of **Ponelle** (**0.8km**).

With the urban experience behind you, follow the asphalt road as it turns to gravel under tall, high-tension power lines and enjoy this relatively flat and wide road, meandering through the small hills and glens of the countryside. The road turns to asphalt again as it climbs to **Scarna** (**1.9km**, fountain, picnic table), then descends and turns back to gravel as it enters woods, soon meeting the official Quartaia option (**0.5km**), which joins from the right.

Official route through Quartaia (15.4km)

Turn right at the option, heading uphill in a southerly direction on a sometimes muddy dirt road under trees. Emerge onto fields before a **derelict bio-gas plant**, then cross the **SR68** roadway. Continue afterward along fields, beginning to climb through woods until you come to an asphalt road, which you cross to walk up to the **Abbazia di Santa Maria Assunta a Conèo** (**3.7km**).

> This simple and beautiful 11th c. **Romanesque chapel** was the heart of a monastery until the 16th c. when it became a parish church. Usually closed due to its location, the buildings were lovingly restored to their Romanesque simplicity in the early 20th c.

A pathway leads back down to the now broken asphalt road, which you follow before turning left to climb through woods. Descend as you come out of the sapling forest into fields, with the dirt road turning to asphalt at the first homes of Quartaia. Follow signs across the **SP27** highway into **Quartaia** (**6.7km**, grocery/ bar). The town's primary medieval monument is its modest Romanesque Church of Sts Jacopo and Filippo.

A shaded dirt road under trees leads out of town, passing a unique, striped stone chapel before continuing alongside a farmhouse. The road gradually turns to asphalt and crosses the Elsa River into the outskirts of **Gracciano dell'Elsa** (**4.8km**, bar, bakery, grocery, pharmacy), a suburb of larger Colle di Val d'Elsa which is

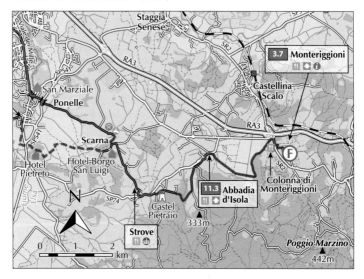

directly to the north. Scholars believe a town near here was Sigeric's Stage XVII, listed by him as Aelse, perhaps a disappeared town named Pieve d'Elsa. A left turn onto the SP451 here would lead you in 700m to the hostel at San Marziale.

Signs point you south along a vestige of the old main street's roadbed before turning left to cross the **SP541** highway and continuing on asphalt in the direction of the **Il Pietreto hotel** (www.hotelpietreto.it/en). Before you reach the hotel, turn left onto a dirt road that circles behind the hotel, heading uphill through fields until just after the **Borgo San Luigi hotel** (www.borgosanluigi.it) you rejoin the recommended route (**3.9km**).

Both routes reunited now, in 100m turn right and follow a straight track uphill into the hamlet of Acquaviva (**0.8km**, no services). The road here turns to asphalt and continues up to the hill of **Strove/San Martino** (**0.9km**, grocery, bar, www.casal-tahotel.com). After town find yourself on a path beside the **SP74** highway, though in a couple hundred meters the signs direct you right at the **Castel Pietraio**, once a castle, then a manor house and now a hotel (www.castelpietraio.it). Another right takes you onto a forest path of red dirt and large white stones, first descending then re-ascending before spilling out into another olive orchard. After the orchard, begin a long descent on a gravel road between olive groves framed by low, stone walls to arrive at **Abbadia d'Isola**.

The façade of the Church of San Cirino shows the subtle Romanesque elements common to this region in the 12th c.

11.3KM ABBADIA D'ISOLA (ELEV 203M, POP 10) 🍴 ⛪ (302.0KM)

In the year 1001 Countess Ava of Staggia founded a monastery dedicated to San Salvatore here when it was called Borgonuovo, a site listed by Sigeric as his Stage XVI. The location was something of an island among swamps that once covered the valley (*Abbadia d'Isola* tr: Abbey of the Island), but its position on the Via Francigena allowed it to dominate pilgrim traffic. A pilgrim hospital cared for Via Francigena travelers as early as 1050. Its current church was consecrated in 1173 to honor San Cirino, and its increasing importance and strategic position between Florence, Siena and other powerful Tuscan towns led in the 14th c. to the building of protective walls. The crown jewel of the site is the 15th c. polyptych altarpiece painted by **Sano di Pietro of Siena**. Many of the buildings surrounding the austere and tranquil Romanesque chapel became farm buildings over the centuries, but have recently been restored for events, conferences and pilgrim hospitality.

⛪ Ospitale San Cirino e Giacomo 🅳🅾 🅺 🆂 6/18, €Donation, Abbadia Isola 4, casaferiesma@yahoo.it or graziellanoni@gmail.com, tel 340 388 1288 or 329 659 3778.

⛪ Ostello Contessa Ava 🅾 🅿🆃 🅳🅾 🆁 🅶🆃 🆂 🆉 10/48, €16/50/60/80, Piazza Garfonda 4 (inside the monumental area), info.contessaava@gmail.com, tel 338 250 6902 or 057 730 0000. €5 discount for pilgrims with +300km walked.

Descend just inside the abbey's main gate to follow a path in the direction of the highway, finding a flat road that makes a slow circuit to the right around a very wide field. Now the walls and towers of Monteriggioni are visible to the right. Come to **Colonna di Monteriggioni** (**3.1km**, restaurants), at the base of the fortress hill. Cross the highway and take the wide gravel path steeply up to the main gate of the walled village of **Monteriggioni** (**0.3km**).

3.7KM MONTERIGGIONI (ELEV 274M, POP 50) 🍴 🛏 ❶ (298.4KM)

One of the most picturesque and beloved places on the Via Francigena, Monteriggioni is a perfectly preserved medieval fortress town standing alone atop a hill covered in vineyards and olive trees. To see its 14 towers and to step inside its fully intact walls is to step back to a day long past. Fearing continual onslaughts by Florence, the city of Siena built the castle of Monteriggioni in the early 13th c. at the perimeter of its defenses. It was scene of many battles and sieges over the centuries and is mentioned in Dante's *Divine Comedy* (Inferno, Canto XXXI). After losing to Florentine forces in the 1269 Battle of Colle, soldiers of Siena hid here to escape death.

Ultimately, both Siena and Florence were incorporated into the Grand Duchy of Tuscany and the fortress became obsolete. Its hilltop location saved it from redevelopment, and it exists as one of Italy's most pristine examples of medieval fortress and village architecture. The roughly circular walls are interrupted at regular intervals by 14 towers. Two gates – one pointing to Florence and one to Siena and Rome – allow access. There is one central street, and medieval and Renaissance-era buildings front onto the street with their gardens behind. The town's simple Romanesque church sits on Piazza Romana, near Porta Romana. A few restaurants, shops and accommodations exist inside the walls, but the space is left quiet each morning and late evening while only a few tourists and pilgrims have the town to themselves (www.monteriggioniturismo.it/en).

Note: the following stage includes a 4–5hr stretch with no food services, so plan accordingly. Check the night before leaving Monteriggioni that the cafés – the only food source in town – will be open by the time you plan to leave.

🛏 **Casa per Ferie Maria Assunta** Ⓞ 🅿f 🅳o 🆁 🅺 🆂 5/20, €20/40/65/-, Piazza Roma 23, casaferiesma@yahoo.it, tel 057 730 4214, 327 065 5678 or 348 325 1628. €5 linens. Reservations required. In heart of historic village.

STAGE 6
Monteriggioni to Siena

Start	Monteriggioni, Piazza Roma
Finish	Siena, Piazza del Campo
Distance	20.6km
Total ascent	514m
Total descent	456m
Difficulty	Moderate
Duration	5¾hr
Percentage paved	42%
Hostels	Siena 20.6km

The first three-quarters of the day is a pleasant and gently undulating walk among forests and farmlands, dotted with medieval castles, but bereft of food services. The last quarter of the day is spent navigating uphill onto the starfish-shaped ridges of Siena. Once inside this world-class Italian hill town, any weariness is forgotten as you marvel that somehow this medieval gem survived the centuries intact. If you can, plan a full day to enjoy Siena's many charms, or at least reserve an afternoon for the Piazza del Campo and Duomo. A Siena pilgrimage completion certificate is available at the cathedral ticket office. The stage includes a 4–5hr stretch with no food services, so plan accordingly. If you have overnighted in Monteriggioni, confirm that the town's cafés will be open by the time you intend to leave.

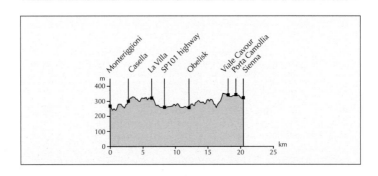

Looking back to the Porta Roma in the medieval walls of Monteriggioni

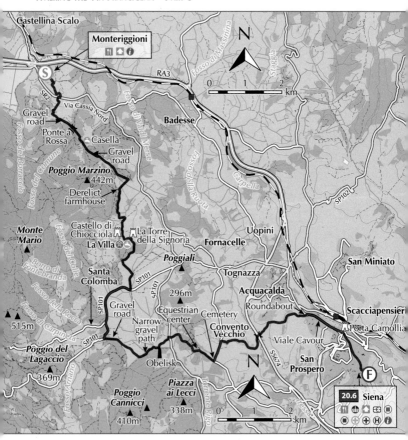

Cross through the Porta Roma at the far end of town, turn right and follow the car road around the parking lot and down the hill, crossing the **SR2 Via Cassia Nord** onto a gravel path as it circumscribes a large field before heading uphill through olive orchards. Looking back, enjoy some excellent views of the walls and towers of Monteriggioni. A left turn takes you onto a **gravel road** that advances across a ridgetop among pastures and woods. Descend to a seasonal creek bed crossed by the **Ponte a Rossa** (**2.2km**) and then veer left to continue on the trail. Foundation stones of the bridge reveal its probable origins during

Roman times. A brief climb brings you to a gravel drive and soon the hamlet of **Casella** (**0.6km**, water fountain).

Continue climbing the hill on the gravel drive through woods and after a time make a hard right off the gravel road onto a two-track gravel path bisecting a large field. Head up toward a **derelict farmhouse** and barn with a castle tower on a ridge to the left. Just before the old farmhouse turn left to traverse the hillside in the direction of the tower. Cross a field and come to a road among scattered buildings, crossing it to arrive just below the **Castello della Chiocciola** castle tower (**3.4km**, B&B, www.torredellachiocciola.it) with its round, turreted stairway. Likely built in the 14th c., this castle is remembered for the heroic stand of its defenders, who combated invading troops here in 1555. Continue along, turning left off the gravel road onto a two-track dirt road taking you toward a square castle tower, **La Torre della Signoria**, on the left at the town of **La Villa** (**0.2km**, pilgrim rest area, water fountain).

Pass in front of the Castello di Villa and alongside another circular tower and begin to descend, turning right on a gravel path. Continue through a wood that abuts open fields as the path forks left. You are now at the edge of the artificially dried lake bed, the Pian del Lago, which you will cross to get to Siena. Continue alongside canals to your left, coming to the **SP101** (**2.0km**) where you turn right to walk on asphalt around the remaining open fields, heading to a low point in the green, wooded ridge ahead. At the far side of the valley, keep left at a fork, continuing on the SP101 as it begins to climb through the woods up onto the ridge. Turn left onto a **gravel road** (**2.0km**) through the woods and begin to descend, bearing left onto a **narrow gravel path** (**1.2km**) leading down through the woods. In an open field, pass a pyramidal **obelisk** (**0.5km**) identifying the 18th c. earthworks that drained the lakebed you have just crossed.

The pyramidal obelisk stands near the entrance to the 2.2km underground Granduca Canal near Siena

At the initiative of Sienese nobleman Francesco Sergardi Bindi, a massive **tunneling project** was undertaken in 1766 to drain the Pian del Lago swamp that was believed to be responsible for malaria outbreaks in the local population. When Bindi's effort fell short, Grand Duke of Tuscany Pietro Leopoldo completed the project, which is a hand-cut brick tunnel of 2m in diameter running for nearly 2.2km to the SE where it empties into Torrente Rigo. The 'Granduca Canale' destroyed the wetland habitat, but created the wide, flat farmland you have just traversed.

Cross an asphalt road and continue up the ridge, generally following the path of the powerlines. Come to an **equestrian center** where the path becomes a gravel drive and then a **cemetery** (**2.2km**) where the gravel turns to asphalt. Turn left to head uphill toward **Convento Vecchio** (**0.6km**, no services). Here turn right onto a gravel drive among modern, brick homes on large lots. Round the mountain, passing a small reservoir below and descend to cross under the **SS674** highway (**1.5km**). Afterward climb steeply up, sometimes between tall, stone walls. Finally come to a **roundabou**t and pharmacy atop the ridge at the **Viale Cavour** (**1.8km**, services), a main road into town, where you turn right. Head among the car-oriented shops through **Porta Camollia** (**1.1km**) into the old town, where the road becomes pedestrian Via Camollia, snaking its way among historic palaces and modern shops directly into the center of **Siena**. Follow signs to walk left down a stairway into the grand and famous Piazza del Campo (**1.3km**).

A brightly clad tourist snaps a photo of the richly decorated façade of the Duomo of Siena

Siena's tall towers stand on the horizon as the path leads out of town

Siena

- 🏛️ Duomo di Siena
- 2️⃣ Baptistry
- 3️⃣ Basilica Cateriniana e San Domenico
- 4️⃣ Santuario Santa Caterina
- 5️⃣ San Donato
- 6️⃣ San Rocco
- 7️⃣ Sant'Andrea

- 🅰️ Siena Hostel Guidoriccio
- 🅱️ Ostello Casa delle Balie - Santa Maria della Scala
- 3️⃣ Santa Luisa Hostel
- 4️⃣ Foresteria San Clemente ai Servi
- ❶ Medici Fortress
- ❷ Santa Maria della Scala
- ❸ Duomo Museum

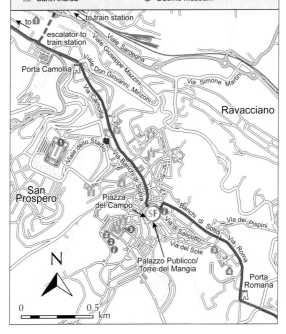

20.6KM SIENA (ELEV 332M, POP 53,937) 🏠 ⊕ 🏛 🄲 🅰 🅱 ⊕ ⊕ 🅗 ➊ (277.8KM)

As one of Italy's best-preserved medieval cities, Siena gives pilgrims (and tourists) a lot to love. Established during Etruscan times, Siena rose to prominence in the Middle Ages, when it jockeyed with Florence for dominance in central Italy. Its population of 60,000 in the late 13th c. was larger than Paris, and its position on the Via Francigena (Sigeric lists it as his Stage XV Seocine) allowed it to control a piece of the important north/south trade on the Via Francigena. Everything changed in 1348 when the Black Death struck down one-third of the city's population. Siena never fully recovered, submitting after centuries to the dominance of Florence, which was content to let it fade into the background. The happy result, though, was the preservation of the town's medieval charm as seen in its long, narrow streets defined by medieval and Renaissance palaces and homes built of brick. Siena further conserved its charm when in 1966 it became one of the first European cities to ban cars in its main square. Beyond enjoying its long lanes and busy piazzas filled with shops and restaurants, Siena has two 'must-see' monuments that can be skimmed in an afternoon, with a deeper dive saved for an additional day.

Piazza del Campo

Originally, a field (*campo* tr: 'field') outside the city walls, this slanted open space became the heart of Siena as its walls were expanded over centuries. At its high point is the 15th c. **Fonte Gaia** (Fountain of Joy) by Jacopo della Quercia, said to have inspired Michelangelo's famous scene at the Sistine Chapel. Its original panels are preserved at the Santa Maria della Scala near the Duomo. Pavement bricks in the piazza are subtly divided to represent the 17th *contrade* (neighborhoods) that compete here in the **Palio horse race** that packs the square with 60,000 spectators twice yearly on July 2 and August 16. At the lower end of the piazza are its most prominent features, the 14th c. **Torre delle Mangia**, at 102m Italy's highest secular tower, and the crenelated and stout **Palazzo Publicco**. The tower allows 50 visitors at a time to climb its 400 steps and enjoy spectacular views from its cantilevered parapet. From here you can see the tower of the Duomo, whose tip reaches the exact same height as the top of the Torre delle Mangia, meant to show the balance between church and state. At the base of the tower is the open-air chapel for the Palio, and to its right is the Palazzo Pubblico, original home of the city's government and now host to the **Museo Comune**. The museum hosts several important works of art, but most famous are the large frescoes by Ambrogio Lorenzetti, the 'Effects of Good and Bad Government' which contain lessons for politicians and voters of any day (€20 ticket gives entry to the Torre, Museo Comune and Santa Maria Scala museum). A full day visit to Siena could include the nearby **Pinacoteca Museum** with its chronological display of Sienese art, including works by Duccio, Martini, Lorenzetti and Beccafumi (€4, Via San Pietro 29, closed Sundays).

Siena Duomo

A few blocks away is one of Italy's most important and beautiful buildings, the 13th c. **Cathedral (Duomo) of Siena** (€5–8, audio guide €3, www.operaduomo. siena.it/en, backpacks are not allowed in the Duomo and can be checked at the Duomo ticket office). The horizontal white and dark marble stripes of the exterior are reminiscent of Pisa and Florence, though here the result is both more grand and more intricate. Crowning the façade's maze of Biblical figures remembered in statuary are three large **Venetian mosaics** – the Coronation of the Virgin in the center, flanked by the Nativity of Jesus and the Presentation of Mary in the Temple. Moving inside, the motif of contrasting horizontal bands is repeated in the nave to a grand, dark and majestic effect. Massive

The interior of the Duomo

piers hold up an immense **dome**, in trompe l'oeil coffering, with golden stars and below them a band of 42 painted patriarchs and prophets. Other works include statues by Donatello, Bernini, and the young Michelangelo. Perhaps the most impressive of all, though, is the mosaic floor of the cathedral, the work of over 40 artists who labored nearly 175 years. Accessible from the nave is the **Piccolomini Library** housing frescoes by Pinturicchio, based on designs by Raphael. Outside and several steps below is the ornate Baptistry – with sculptures by Donatello and others – and frescoed **crypt**, located under the cathedral's altar area. Many of the cathedral's original artworks are preserved in an interesting display at the **Museo dell'Opera e Panorama**, next to the Duomo (€6 possible combined ticket with Duomo) that also features a brilliant view over the cathedral complex as well as some of the arched remnants of the grander cathedral plan that was begun but never completed. With extended time in Siena, across the piazza from the Duomo is the **Santa Maria della Scala museum** with its splendid frescoes and displays of art and archeological finds from Siena's long history (€6, possible to combine with Torre and Comune tickets).

San Domenico and Catherine of Siena

An extended visit to Siena would have to include a stop at the **Church of San Domenico**, an enormous, but austere brick structure of the Dominican order, a member of which was Saint Catherine of Siena, co-patron saint of Italy. In the scant 33 years of her life (1347–1380) this youngest of 25 children became one of Italy's most revered mystics. San Domenico exhibits some of her relics – a thumb and her skull – while the Church of Santa Maria Sopra Minerva in Rome holds the rest. The church has a series of paintings depicting her life, which is also remembered nearby at the **Sanctuary of St Catherine**, a heavily embellished building that once was her family's home (free, open daily, Costa di Sant'Antonio 6).

🛏 Accoglienza Santa Luisa **O Do R Br Dr S** 4/20, €Donation, Via dei Servi 4, acc. santaluisam@libero.it, tel 057 728 4377 or 057 720 1271.

🛏 Comunità Santa Regina **O Pr Do R K S Z** 27/51, €Donation, Via Bianca Piccolomini Clementini 6, tel 057 722 1206. Approx 3km E of Siena.

🛏 Foresteria San Clemente ai Servi **O Do R K** 6/20, €Donation, Piazza Manzoni 5, weabis1233@gmail.com, tel 057 722 2633 or 389 298 3135.

🛏 Ostello Santa Maria della Scala (aka Casa di Belie) **O Do R** 5/25, €18/-/-/-, Vicolo San Girolamo, online reservations **www.santamariadellascala.com/it/ostello**, tel 347 613 7678. Daytime check-in at tourist office in Piazza Duomo.

🛏 Siena Hostel Guidoriccio **O Pr Do R Br Gr W S Z** 42/110, €23/30/50/75, Via Fiorentina 89, info@sienahostel.it, tel 057 716 98177. Tourist hostel. Bike rental and bus service to central Siena.

🛏 A Casa di Sabri **O Pr R K Br Do W S** 1/2, €-/-/40/-, Viale Mazzini 36, sabrina. erdas76@gmail.com, tel 340 604 7608.

🏕 Camping Siena Colleverde **Pr R K Gr W** 95/154, €-/30/50/-, Strada di Scacciapensieri 47, info@sienacamping.com, tel 057 733 4080. Tent camping available. Less then 1km NE of train station.

STAGE 7
Siena to Ponte d'Arbia

Start	Siena Piazza, del Campo
Finish	Ponte d'Arbia, Centro Cresti
Distance	25.9km
Total ascent	391m
Total descent	572m
Difficulty	Moderate
Duration	7hr
Percentage paved	44%
Hostels	Ponte d'Arbia 25.9km

The joys of medieval Siena quickly fade and are replaced by the quiet of vast farmlands, dotted with small hamlets and farmhouses. Red Sienese farmland is replaced by Crete Senesi – gray, claylike soil – that gives its name to this region that extends south of Siena through Monteroni d'Arbia. The stretch between Isola d'Arbia and Ponte d'Arbia includes two off-track options for refreshment, but otherwise there are no services for the 16km between the two.

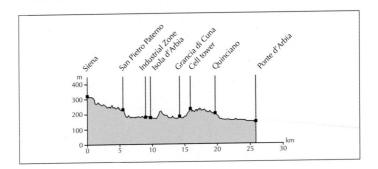

In the Piazza del Campo, face the Mangia Tower and head left onto Via Rinaldini. Turn right when it ends in one block and find yourself on Via Banchi di Sotto, one of Siena's main pedestrian streets. Continue along the street as it becomes Via Roma and exits the old city through the Porta Romana (**1.0km**). Just after the city gate, turn left and head downhill on an asphalt lane. Soon cross the SR2, your first

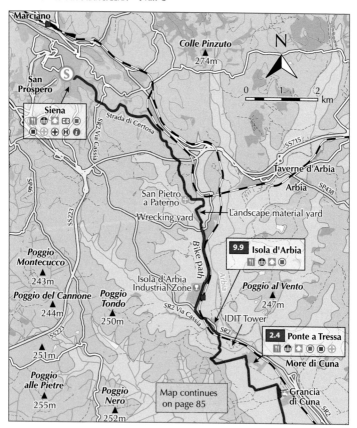

of many encounters with the historic Via Cassia, originally built by the Romans to connect Rome and Florence. On the other side of the SR2, continue downhill in the same direction on this road, called the **Strada di Certosa**, which descends between stone and brick walls.

The road branches right and you follow it through olive orchards and among homes with tall iron fences as Siena fades in the background. Just before the 11th c. **Church of San Pietro a Paterno** (**4.5km**) the road turns left and switches to gravel, now descending more steeply. At the bottom of the hill make a right turn onto a gravel **bike/pedestrian path**, descending to an asphalt lane between a **wrecking**

yard and **landscape material yard**. Follow the road over a roundabout and continue on the bike path. Turn left onto the highway and continue through car dealerships and warehouses with loud, heavy trucks thundering by into the **Industrial Zone of Isola d'Arbia** (3.2km, bar). Although some GPS tracks have you turn left to follow the railroad tracks, that path is now disused and overgrown, so instead follow the road to the next intersection and turn left to walk along the **Via Cassia** into town.

9.9KM ISOLA D'ARBIA (ELEV 174M, POP 1060) 🏨 ⊕ ⛺ ◉ (267.9KM)

This hamlet is called Isola (tr: 'island') d'Arbia due to its one-time isolation between the Arbia and Tressa rivers. Today a wide spot on the Via Cassia, its historic roots are evident in the modest but venerable Romanesque **Church of Sant'Ilario**. Economic development projects in the late 20th c. brought the industrial zone to its northern edge and also the tall metal and concrete tower of the IDIT project, intended for freeze-drying of tomatoes but never finished.

⌂ Guesthouse Il Pozzo Ⓞ Pr Ⓡ Ⓒ 5/8, €-/40/60/-, Via Cassia Sud 302, info@sangiorgio.net, 348 054 1474, 349 395 933

As you enter town, fork right off the highway at the first bar and walk through a neighborhood of newer homes of brick and concrete. The road veers back toward the highway and you follow it briefly, before turning right, crossing under the railroad tracks and forking left as the road turns to gravel and heads out into the fields, finding Crete Sinesi scenery of rolling hills and cypress trees, before heading back toward the highway. The route turns right a few blocks before the commercial center of **Ponte a Tressa**.

2.4KM PONTE A TRESSA (ELEV 191M, POP 1353) 🏨 ⊕ ⛺ ◉ ◉ ⊕ (265.5KM)

Located at the confluence of the Tressa and Arbia rivers, the town hosted a pilgrim hospital as early as 1215. Its primary contemporary link to medieval times is its 15th **Church of San Michele Arcangelo**. (Train: www.trenitalia.com. Bus: www.tiemmespa.it.)

⌂ Il Gelso Ⓞ Pr Ⓓo Ⓡ Ⓚ Ⓢ 2/3, €-/35/70/-, Piazza della Cisterna 71, ilgelso71@gmail.com, tel 334 819 0664.

Now continue straight among the fields of alfalfa and grain (or grey soil after harvest) until a left turn at a sign that says 'Private Property.' The road takes you to the large, brick complex of **Grancia di Cuna** (1.9km, water).

A tower stands on the outer walls of La Grancia di Cuna fortified farm

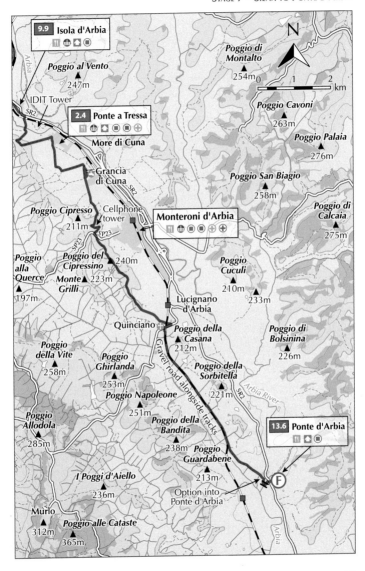

La Grancia di Cuna is one of Tuscany's best-preserved **fortified farms** (*grancia* tr: 'fortified farm'). Set up originally as an arm of the Abbey di Torri in the 12th c., when the area came under Sienese rule in the 13th c. it was connected with the pilgrim hospital of Santa Maria della Scala in Siena. Its buildings include the 12th/13th c. Church of San Jacopo e Cristoforo, which has a fresco with a scene of the hanged man of Santo Domingo on the Camino de Santiago. The walls, houses and fortifications of the complex range from the 12th to 17th c. Cuna was sacked in 1554 by Austrian-Spanish troops, but in its heyday gave refuge to kings, popes and Via Francigena pilgrims.

After Cuna the road circles down and meets an asphalt road, where you turn left alongside modern duplex-style homes. Follow signs leading first on roads and then onto a narrow path that climbs to a tall **cellphone tower** from which you can enjoy wide vistas over the countryside. Head down the hill and turn right onto a gravel road heading toward the **SP23** asphalt road (**2.3km**), which has the easier entry into the largest town in the area, **Monteroni d'Arbia** (**1.2km off track**, food, groceries, bus, train, clinic). After this town there are no services until Ponte d'Arbia in 9.4km.

A new pedestrian bridge crosses the Arbia River just before Ponte d'Arbia

A series of farm roads in rolling hills, often with wide territorial views now lead to the hamlet of **Quinciano** (**3.2km**) with its large *palazzo*, monumental stairway, and 19th c. octagonal Chapel of Pieri Nerli. The road turns to asphalt as you descend to the highway, where you turn right, following the roadway for just 200m before turning left and heading down to a **gravel road** that follows alongside the train tracks among fields of sunflowers. Walk this road for 3.6km, first on the right and then on the left side of the tracks, finally veering to the left and arriving at an option (**1.5km**). At a hard right on the outskirts of **Ponte d'Arbia** you can turn left and walk 150m to town for refreshment or turn right to walk 400m across the new pilgrim/pedestrian bridge over the Arbia River to the Centro Cresti pilgrim hostel (**0.4km**) for a bed. The beautiful, but dangerously narrow Via Cassia automobile bridge also spans the river here.

13.6KM PONTE D'ARBIA (ELEV 149M, POP 472) 🏧 🔼 ◉ (251.9KM)

Located at the crossing of the Arbia River and the Via Cassia, this tiny but ancient village was Stage XIV of Sigeric, originally called 'Borgo d'Arbia,' but famous for its 14th/17th c. bridge of five wide arches. Its medieval structures were almost entirely leveled in an Allied bombing of 1944, which aimed at the bridge but damaged most everything nearby except its target. Today the village is a loose cluster of mostly modern buildings, scattered on both sides of the river. One of its oldest buildings is the 1840 **Centro Cresti**, which has variously been a series of workshops, a nursery school, housing for Indochinese refugees and, since 1983, a pilgrim hostel on the Via Francigena.

⌂ Centro Cresti ◉ ⒹⓄ ℝ Ⓚ Ⓦ ⓢ 4/20, €Donation, Via Cassia 3, **www.centro-cresti.it**, centrocresti@libero.it, tel 327 719 7439.

⌂ Affittacamere Martelli ◉ ℙⓡ ℝ Ⓑⓡ Ⓦ ⓢ 3/9, €-/30/40/60, SS Cassia km 204, martellao1958@alice.it, tel 057 780 6262, 348 746 3634 or 334 846 4235 (English). On the river at a former mill. Call the day before.

STAGE 8
Ponte d'Arbia to San Quirico d'Orcia

Start	Ponte d'Arbia, Centro Cresti
Finish	San Quirico d'Orcia, Parish of Santi Quirico e Giulitta
Distance	26.2km
Total ascent	807m
Total descent	541m
Difficulty	Moderately hard
Duration	7½hr
Percentage paved	24%
Hostels	Buonconvento 4.4km, Torrenieri 18.5km, San Quirico d'Orcia 26.2km

A few steep hills make this a tougher than average stage, but if the weather is clear you will remember it less for its hills than for its stunning views of Tuscan countryside, particularly up toward Montalcino among the Brunello vineyards and at stage end toward San Quirico d'Orcia. Buonconvento is a charming and historic coffee stop or alternate overnight, while Torrenieri comes at just the right time for an afternoon break.

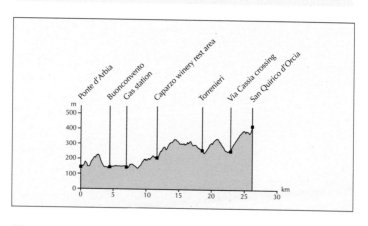

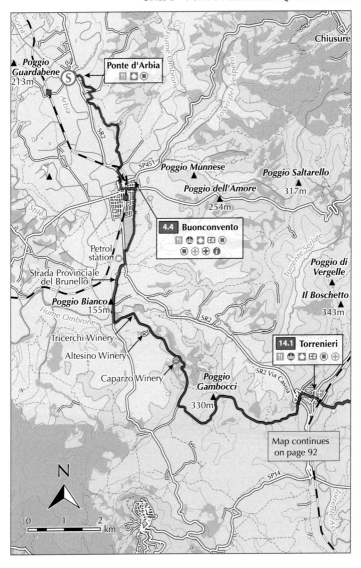

Map continues on page 92

At the hostel, turn uphill and follow the gravel road onto a series of roads and paths that keep you among fields and off the SR2, touching the road briefly once for a few moments before turning back uphill with the climb becoming somewhat steep toward the top. The road then turns right and heads to the crest of the next hill, gradually veering right as it heads back toward the highway. Turn left when you reach the **SR2 Via Cassia** just before town and cross the **River Ombrone** on the highway bridge. Just afterward, turn right to enter historic **Buonconvento** at its Porta Sienese.

Morning mist shrouds the Torre dell'Orologio and the tower of Santi Pietro e Paolo in Buonconvento

4.4KM BUONCONVENTO (ELEV 152M, POP 3102)
🚉 ⊕ ⌂ 🄲 ⊚ ◉ ⊕ ⊕ ❶ (247.5KM)

Some people call Buonconvento one of the most beautiful villages in Italy, and ambling down Via Soccini it is hard to disagree; after all, the name Buonconvento comes from the Latin *bonus conventus* for 'happy place.' The historic medieval center is remarkably well preserved and while blessedly not as touristic as some other medieval Italian towns, it still brims with cafés, restaurants and shops. The town was first mentioned in records from the year 1100, while its walls date from the 14th c. and most of its grand homes are from the Renaissance period. The village earned its place in history when, in 1313 as the armies of the Holy Roman Empire were besieging Siena, Emperor Henry VII died here from malaria. His body was taken for burial in the Pisa cathedral. The **Museo d'Arte Sacra** (€3, Via Soccini 18) houses local religious artworks from the 14th–18th c., while the **Museo della Mezzadria** (Museum of Sharecropping) shows what life was like for farmworkers in past centuries (€3, Piazzale Garibaldi). Consult online resources for available hotels.

Continue through the old town and, just after the next city gate turn left, heading back to cross the highway and the railroad tracks, continuing until just before a hill where you make a right turn onto a gravel path leading behind a schoolyard. Pass the schoolyard into a suburban neighborhood among apartment

Cypress trees surround the Altesino Winery near Montalcino

blocks. The road becomes a path which ends at a small vineyard across a concrete road going downhill to the highway. Cross the SR2 onto a path on the opposite side, just beyond the guardrail. Pass a **petrol station** (2.6km, café) and turn right as the path follows the **Strada Provinciale del Brunello** leading uphill. The path reaches a summit and turns left to continue climbing, with vineyards of prized Brunello di Montalcino grapes on the right and the buildings of the **Tricerchi Winery** complex (www.castellotricerchi.com) at the summit. Now begin downhill, looking back to see distant views of Buonconvento and views above to Montalcino, capital of Brunello wines.

> **Brunello di Montalcino wines** are considered some of Italy's best and certainly its most expensive wines. First mentioned in the 14th c. and originally thought to be a separate grape variety, in 1879 it was determined that Brunello vines are actually Sangiovese. Vintages benefit from the hot and dry sub-climate of this region and strict requirements must be met to earn the Brunello DOCG appellation.

A pleasant gauntlet of cypresses leads past the **Altesino Winery** (www.winbow.com) to the **Caparzo Winery** (4.6km, rest area, www.caparzo.it). After a left in about 20 minutes, continue on the road for quite some time, distracted by majestic views of Tuscan countryside on the right and left as the road curls its way along the ridges. A town appears on the left and the gravel road ends at the SR2 highway just before it. A right turn leads to the center of **Torrenieri**.

14.1KM TORRENIERI (ELEV 259M, POP 1600) 🏨 ⊕ 🏠 🄴 ⊚ ⊕ (233.3KM)

A castle at 'Turreiner' is believed to have stood here as early as the 9th–10th c., and its existence is documented in 990 as Sigeric's Stage XIII Turreiner. Its name was either derived from its founder, Ranieri, Lord of San Quirico (torre-ranieri tr: 'tower of Ranieri') or perhaps from the effects of fire on its battlements (torre-neri tr: 'black tower'). In the Middle Ages its regional importance arose from its position on the Via Francigena between the Orcia and Arbia valleys. With few natural defenses, the town was often sacked by passing armies, including a 1235 pillage and conflagration by the army of Orvieto. In the 14th and 15th c. Siena strengthened the walls here, using it as one of its territorial defenses, but with the fall of the Republic of Siena and the rise of Florence, over the next centuries the town drifted into obscurity. Documents record a pilgrim hospital dedicated to Sant'Antonio here in 1606, and an evocative bronze sculpture of pilgrim feet arranged like a bouquet stands adjacent to the 19th c. Church of Santa Maria Maddalena.

🛖 **Pellegrinaio del Poggio** 🄿🅃 🄳🄾 🅁 🄺 🅂 4/10, €15/15/30/45, Via Cesare Battisti 37, Giuseppe.antichi@libero.it, tel 348 737 2473 or 342 941 5024. Linen €5.

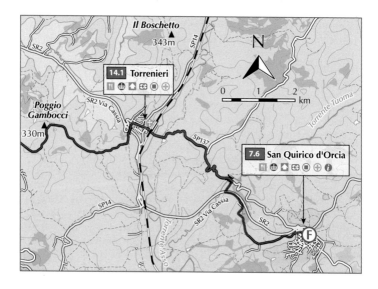

Continue downhill past the church, aiming toward the bottom of the valley. This quiet asphalt road, the Strada Provinciale Celamonti (**SP137**), will carry you the next hour, making a long and gradual climb to a summit. As you descend you can now see the outline of San Quirico on a ridge between two hills ahead. Reach the bottom of the valley and cross a bridge before taking a right turn on a gravel road (**4.0km**) heading toward the Via Cassia. As it starts to ascend it curls under the highway overpass (**0.4km**) and begins to make a steep and sustained climb. Pass through olive orchards, alongside a farmhouse and then through woods. The road dips and then continues up again, crossing under an archway of an old road above. Climb a final flight of steps and turn left toward the Collegiate Church of Saints Quirico and Giulitta (**3.3km**) which is the start of the pleasant pedestrian walk through this historic town.

7.6KM SAN QUIRICO D'ORCIA (ELEV 415M, POP 2672)
🏨 ⊕ 🛏 🄲 ◉ ⊕ ❶ (225.7KM)

This beloved and atmospheric walled village is capital of a region that in 2004 was declared a UNESCO world heritage site. An important stop along the Via Francigena (it was Sigeric's Stage XII Sce Quiric), the town famously hosted an important meeting between Emperor Federico I Barbarossa and Papal legates in 1155. San Quirico d'Orcia bears the name of Syrian St Cyricus (Italian: Quirico), who along with his mother, St Julitta, were 4th c. martyrs. They are remembered at the 12th c. **Collegiate Church** named in their honor. The church has a remarkable Romanesque main portal, with sculptures of lions, alligators, other animals, and plants. Its side portal is said to have been the work of Giovanni Pisano, overseer of the Siena Duomo. The 11th c. **Church of Santa Maria Assunta**, standing at the other end of pedestrian Via Dante Alighieri, is a gem of Romanesque architecture. Between the two, at the Piazza della Libertà, stands the Church of San Francesco that houses a Madonna by famed 16th c. sculptor Andrea della Robbia. The symmetrical **Horti Leonini gardens** date from 1561 and carefully pruned hedges radiate around a 1688 statue of Cosimo III de'Medici.

🛏 Ostello Parrocchia Collegiata 🄾 🄳🄾 🅁 🄺 🅂 5/27, €13/-/-/-, Piazza Chigi 1–18, casaferie@parrsanquiricodorcia.it, tel 328 132 9899 or 057 789 7236. Check-in 15:30–18:30. Sheets €5, towels €3.

🛏 Il Palazzo del Pellegrino 🄾 🄳🄾 🅁 🅂 3/18, €10/-/-/-, Via Dante Alighieri 33, ufficioturistico@comune.sanquiricodorcia.si.it, tel 057 789 9728.

STAGE 9
San Quirico d'Orcia to Radicofani

Start	San Quirico d'Orcia, Collegiate Church
Finish	Radicofani, Chiesa di Santa Maria Assunta
Distance	32.9km
Total ascent	1164m
Total descent	790m
Difficulty	Hard
Duration	9¾hr
Percentage paved	25%
Hostels	Passalacqua Agriturismo 16.9km, Radicofani 32.9km, Abbadia San Salvatore 35.1km

This scenic walk is one of the harder stages of the Via Francigena due to length but more importantly because of the 12km of constant uphill at the end. Plan your food and water carefully since fountains and food stops are limited and distances are long. The only refreshment directly on the route between Bagno Vignoni and Radicofani is an *agriturismo* near Gallina. Otherwise a saunter into Gallina is 1.1km off the track. If you're able, save some energy at stage end for the 1km hike up to Rocca Radicofani and its epic view over the region. This stage also includes a hilly variant through historic Abbadia San Salvatore that misses Radicofani.

Continue to the end of Via Dante Alighieri, San Quirico's pedestrian street, and turn right at the first street with vehicle access, Via Matteoti. In a couple of blocks fork left onto Via Garibaldi, which will take you through a neighborhood of suburban homes and then into fields framed by pine and cypress trees. At a **Y-junction (1.2km)** the road turns to gravel and climbs, sometimes steeply, though the 15% gradient posted on the sign seems an exaggeration. Soon a vista of Rocca d'Orcia with its rectangular castle tower appears on the right. Come to a **rest area** and kiosk on the right and not long afterward reach the summit of the climb. On a hilltop far across the valley, you can now see the tall tower of the fortress at Radicofani, the goal for the day.

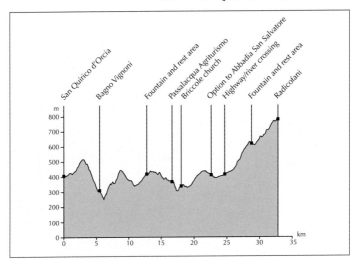

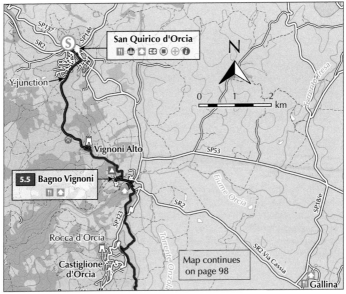

The road turns to concrete as it descends, but arrows point you left onto gravel to enter the picturesque castle/hamlet of **Vignoni Alto** (**2.4km**), sentry site for Bagno Vignoni below. Walk through the archway for an iconic view of the Tuscan countryside, and then down the path to catch the gravel road once again. The road turns to concrete and begins to descend very steeply. Pass a campground and at the start of the bath complex turn right onto a concrete path to make your way to the Piazza delle Sorgenti (tr: 'Square of Springs') in **Bagno Vignoni**, surrounded by small hotels, a bar and the Church of San Giovanni Batista.

Two Italian pilgrims at an archway of Vignoni that overlooks the Val d'Orcia

5.5KM BAGNO VIGNONI (ELEV 314M, POP 30) ⦚ ⦚ (220.2KM)

Archeological research shows the hot springs of Bagno Vignoni have been enjoyed since at least Etruscan times. Largely unchanged since the Middle Ages, the springs were frequented by medieval notables such as St Catherine of Siena, Pope Pius II and Lorenzo the Magnificent. The 16th c. central square is a cluster of picturesque buildings surrounding a pool of spring-fed hot water, making it the only aquatic piazza in Italy (sadly, no swimming here). The spring waters flow out toward the Orcia River, passing the **Mulini Natural Park** where four medieval mills, carved into the cliffside, once ground local seed into flour. Consult online resources for available hotels.

Turn left just after the main pool and head straight past the parking lot. Just 50m before the stop sign turn right onto a gravel road that descends to cross the majestic wooden bridge over the **Orcia River**. Climb up after the bridge past a posh hotel (www.osteriadellorcia.com), turning right afterward onto a dirt and gravel path that circles up around a field, leading up to a house where the gravel path widens to a gravel road. Cross the **SP323** asphalt road and then a small vineyard and orchard with Rocca d'Orcia straight ahead. After the orchard, the route turns a hard left onto a gravel road that traverses the hillside and then

Mist rises from the warm waters of Bagno Vignoni's famous Piazza dell'Acqua

crosses through fields with **Castiglione d'Orcia** on the right. Come up alongside a road briefly and then double back to go steeply up a deeply rutted dirt road. The road soon levels out with a wide view of the d'Orcia valley to the left. In a few moments, merge with a road that comes from the right and immediately take a path up to the right to find another gravel road, a wider one, that descends between vineyards. This is the road that will lead you much of the way toward the bottom of the wide valley.

At first a descent carries you through olive orchards and woods full of birdsong, with few homes in the area. Cross a bridge over **Torrente Onzola** (5.5km) and then a second bridge right afterward. After a climb, the road breaks out into the open, with fields on both sides. Keep left as a road forks off to the right and then begin to climb. As you continue to climb, turn a hard left onto a gravel road that leads left through a field finding in about 100m **Agriturismo Antonio** (**1.9km**, water). Continue to an unmarked option (**1.4km**) where a left fork in the road would take you directly into **Gallina**, the only intermediate stop for services between Bagno Vignoni and Radicofani. Directly on the Via Cassia, the hamlet of Gallina is 1.1km off the walking track at its closest (bar, restaurant, ⌂ Ostello La Vecchia Posta 🅿 🅳 🆁 🅺 🆆 🆂, 2/10 €15/-/40/60, Via Cassia 43/45, lavecchiaposta@yahoo.com, tel 331 997 2594 or 339 105 0576. Bed linens and towel €5. ⌂ B&B da Nonna Ornella 🅾 🅳 🆁 🅺 🅱 🅳 🆆 🆂 🆉, 1/3, €-/40/-/-, Le Querciole 9, diva.orfei@gmail.com, tel 392 808 4706 or 320 184 8695.)

Continue on and come to another fork, where you can either turn left, again toward Gallina, or, to stay on the route, turn right just before **Agriturismo Passalacqua** (**2.6km**, lunch and accommodation available for pilgrims,  Agriturismo Passalacqua Pr R K Br Dr Cf W S Z, 8/16, €-/45/90/135, Strada Vicinale di Passalacqua 1, info@agriturismopassalacqua.it, tel 335 547 0868 or 320 792 2988. 100% organic farm directly on path). The road continues down toward the **SR2 Via Cassia** at the bottom of the hill where you turn right to walk up among vast fields of hay or alfalfa in season heading toward high-tension power lines. Follow trail markings to the historic **Church of San Pellegrino at Briccole** (**1.3km**).

Archbishop Sigeric rested at this once-flourishing **abbey** on the Via Francigena as his Stage XI Abricula. In its 13th c. heyday the abbey saw visitors as prominent as Kings Philippe Auguste and Charles d'Anjou. The tiny, unrestored chapel is most all that remains, with just a few architectural hints visible of its Romanesque lineage.

After the church, the road turns to grass and runs alongside a large pasture. Cross the asphalt **SP del Banditone** near the bottom of the valley and then a seasonal creek just afterward, continuing on the grassy road. After the grassy track turns to gravel it ends at the roadway of the **Old Via Cassia**, where you turn right and pass alongside **Agriturismo Sant'Alberto** (**1.3km**, pilgrim rest area, www.santalberto.

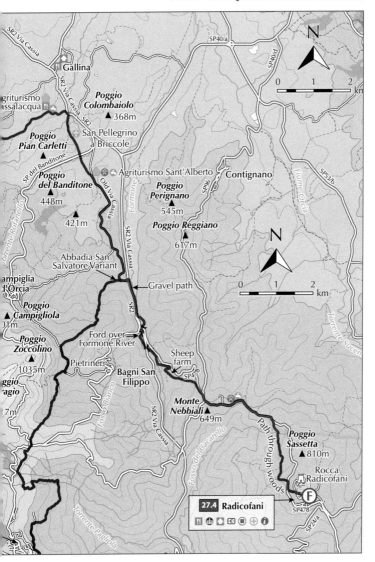

All that is left of a once prosperous pilgrim hospital at Briccole is the small, Romanesque church of San Pellegrino

com). Go left at a fork and begin a long and sustained climb on broken asphalt. The road heads downhill and ends at the new SR2 Via Cassia (**3.6km**) in a wide intersection. Here the variant through San Salvatore (see description below) takes off to the right, climbing back up toward the south slope of Monte Amiata rather than crossing the Via Cassia.

For the main route, carefully cross the highway and follow the gravel path to the right, between the highway and the Formone River. A marble sign soon correctly indicates the distance to Radicofani as 8km. The path crosses under the **SP478** bridge first, and as you cross under the SR2 afterward you also ford the river (**1.6km**) on large, white stones, taking you briefly to the east side of the SR2. The path crosses back under the highway, comes to a home marked 'Private Property,' and then leads left on a long and sustained climb, first up the hill next to a **sheep farm** and then as you turn right onto the **SP478** highway (**3.1km**).

For the next few kilometers climb uphill on a narrow pathway to the left of the road that shields you from cars zooming down the highway, with peekaboo views of the tall tower of Rocca Radicofani above. Pass a fountain and rest area (**1.1km**) and in the midst of a highway curve take a right turn onto a path (**1.4km**) that makes a beeline for town. Follow it down through woods and then up, enjoying views to the right of tall Monte Amiata. The path ends at the highway (**2.0km**)

Via Roma in medieval Radicofani

where you turn right and in 200m find a road on the left that leads to the compact grey/brown stone buildings of central **Radicofani** (0.7km).

27.4KM RADICOFANI (ELEV 793M, POP 1088) 🏠 ⊕ ⛺ Ⓔ ◉ ⊕ ❶ (192.8KM)

Radicofani is best known as location for the tall **fortress** above the village that has dominated the countryside since at least the 9th c. Standing astride a high ridge between Tuscany and Lazio, the fortress was long a key strategic point in the conquest or defense of central Italy. In 978 the monks of Abbazia San Salvatore bought the fortress to defend their properties and protect travelers on the Via Francigena. In the mid-12th c. the Papal States strengthened its fortifications to guard against the advance of Frederick Barbarossa, and it passed at various times into the hands of either Siena or the Papal States. The famous Sienese 'gentleman bandit,' Ghino di Tacco, took possession in 1297 and from here made raids on the Papal States and on bands of unsuspecting and innocent Via Francigena pilgrims. Though he robbed them of their treasures, he always invited them afterward to join him for plentiful banquets in his home. While the Papal States saw him as a scoundrel, his raids against papal properties earned him clemency from punishment in his native Siena. In Radicofani he is remembered in the **Piazza di Ghino di Tacco** off the Via Roma. The 16th c. saw the waning of Sienese influence, and

101

the castle keys were handed to Cosimo I, Florentine Grand Duke of Tuscany, who set about improving the castle's defenses. Angered at his removal as its commander, in 1735 Piero of Piancastagnaio destroyed the fortress with gunpowder, and it lay in ruins until its restoration in the last decades of the 20th c. (€4, bar, restaurant, open daily in season 10:00–20:00, www.fortezzadiradicofani.it/eng). The village of Radicofani itself is a picturesque cluster of neat, stone homes, shops and restaurants, and at its heart is the **Romanesque Church of San Pietro** (reconstructed after damage in WWII bombings), which includes glazed terracottas from the workshop of Andrea della Robbia.

🏠 **Rifugio Comunale 'A. Gestri'** Ⓞ ⒟ⓞ Ⓡ Ⓦ Ⓢ 5/44, €14/-/-/-, Piazza Garibaldi 2, infostelloradicofani@libero.it, tel 331 529 1556.

🏠 **Spedale Santi Pietro e Giacomo** Ⓞ ⒟ⓞ Ⓚ Ⓑⓕ Ⓓⓡ Ⓢ 3/16, €Donation, Via dello Spedale 2, tel 338 798 2255 or 331 532 1867. Open summers or by request. Breakfast and dinner possible in summer by reservation.

Variant: San Quirico d'Orcia to Acquapendente via Abbadia San Salvatore

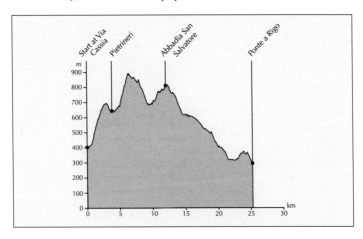

Though Sigeric almost certainly passed through Abbadia San Salvatore, which he listed ambiguously as Stage X Sce Petir in Pail, the modern stewards of the Via Francigena have wisely listed the challenging route to modern Abbadia San

Salvatore as a variant. This variant adds 5km to the distance to Acquapendente (Stage 10), with a 956m ascent and 1064m descent.

The track begins where the main route crosses the Via Cassia after Gallina, taking a very steep trail up the hillside on a forested path. Climb 300m first to **Pietrineri** (3.8km) and then surmount two more tall hills to arrive at the historic town of **Abbadia San Salvatore** (8.3km).

29.7KM ABBADIA SAN SALVATORE (ELEV 813M, POP 6275)
🏨 ⊕ 🛒 🅲 ⊙ ⊕ ❶ (195.6KM)

In the early Middle Ages this prosperous abbey on the slopes of Monte Amiata dominated commerce in the Paglia valley, holding sway over Radicofani and serving as a bulwark between powerful Siena, Orvieto and the Papal States until it finally was conquered by Siena in 1265. For centuries the abbey library held the **Northumbrian Codex Amiatinus**, the oldest complete copy of the Latin Vulgate Bible, finished in 716 in Britain and intended as a gift for Pope Gregory II. How this precious book ended up here is a mystery. Commissioned by Abbot Ceolfrid of the Monkwearmouth-Jarrow Monastery in Northumbria in 692, it was to be hand-delivered to the Pope in 716 by Ceolfrid himself. However, the abbot died in Burgundy en route to Rome and the manuscript disappeared for 300 years. The first evidence of its whereabouts is in a list of Abbazia San Salvatore's relics dated 1036. The immense illuminated manuscript weighs over 34kg (75lb) and since 1786 has been kept at the Laurentian Library in Florence. (Bus: to Acquapendente, 45min, 4 times daily, https://servizi.cotralspa.it.)

🛏 Abbazia del Santissimo Salvatore 🅾 🆍 🆁 🆂, 1/4, €Donation, Via del Monastero 50, abbazia.sansalvatore@virgilio.it, tel 057 777 7352. Closed on major holidays.

Descend after town on the gravel surface of the SP dei Combattenti leading downhill among fields, then industrial estates, and crossing the **SR2 Via Cassia** into **Ponte a Rigo** (13km) to rejoin the main route to Aquapendente from Radicofani, 10.5km into Stage 10.

STAGE 10
Radicofani to Acquapendente

Start	Radicofani, Chiesa di Santa Maria Assunta
Finish	Acquapendente, Piazza Fabrizio
Distance	23.1km (31.3km via Proceno)
Total ascent	392m (708m via Proceno)
Total descent	801m (1117m via Proceno)
Difficulty	Moderate
Duration	6¼hr
Percentage paved	41%
Hostels	Ponte a Rigo 10.5km, Acquapendente 23.1km (21.5km Proceno)

After a long and quiet downhill on a good and scenic gravel road, the official route points you onto six harrowing kilometers of the car-centric Via Cassia. The only alternatives are to take a bus or hire a taxi at Centeno, to continue on foot by walking the longer alternative route through lovely Proceno, or to fight the cars by walking the road anyway.

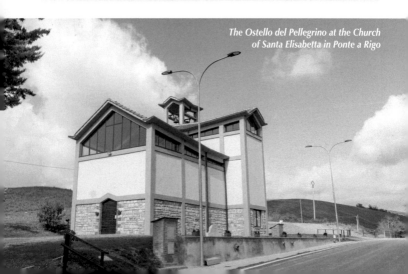

The Ostello del Pellegrino at the Church of Santa Elisabetta in Ponte a Rigo

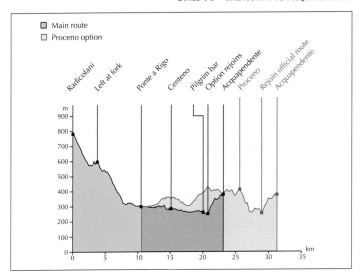

Take the main pedestrian street, the Via Roma, downhill through the lower city gate and go straight onto the **SP24** road leading downhill. Cross the **SP478** highway (**0.8km**) and continue straight ahead. In just 200m fork left on the wide, gravel Ex-Via Cassia that takes you on a long and scenic descent toward the valley floor. Look back in good weather to see the tower of Radicofani and left and right to see views over hayfields toward mountain ridges. Pass the Agriturismo Podere Pantano (www.poderepantano.it/en), and as the bottom nears, go through a farm and then a large **estate**, passing the Francigena B&B (see www.booking.com) and finally reaching the valley floor. The road undulates for a time, finding a hillside just above the river before coming to **Ponte a Riga** and the Via Cassia. Here the variant from Abbadia San Salvatore rejoins the main route.

10.5KM PONTE A RIGO (ELEV 293M, POP 55) 🏨 🏕 ◉ (182.3KM)

Known originally as 'Borgo a Rigo' and documented as early as 1074, the town today has little evidence of its medieval lineage. (Bus: 20min to Acquapendente, 2 times daily, https://servizi.cotralspa.it.)

⛺ **Casa del Pellegrino** ◉ ➍ Ⓡ Ⓢ ⓩ 2/8, €Donation, Celle sul Rigo 320, tel 339 361 1055 or 334 354 6142. At Santa Elisabetta parish.

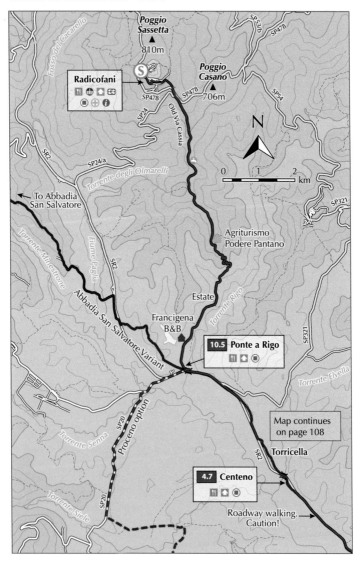

Here you are faced with a choice. If you turn left on the official route to cross the Rigo, six of the next 10km (from Centeno to the pilgrim bar) have you dodging speeding vehicles on the pavement of the Via Cassia. A longer, harder and more scenic option is to walk the alternate route through Proceno.

Alternate route via Proceno (additional 8km to Acquapendente)
At Ponte a Rigo turn right onto a pathway on the far side of the Via Cassia and follow the path as it turns off the Via Cassia and onto the **SP20** minor road (**0.6km**). When the path ends, walk on the quiet SP20 itself for several kilometers gradually uphill among farms. Follow the sign to turn left (**4.4km**) before a farmhouse complex onto a gravel road among fields. Descend on rough gravel, crossing a seasonal stream and passing farmhouses. The road turns to broken asphalt and you make a right turn after a **dairy farm** (**5.9km**). Continue following the signs as you climb to the Proceno **cemetery** (**3.3km**), where you veer right onto an asphalt road. Soon come to **Proceno**, where the signs lead you to the Piazza della Libertà at the heart of town.

15.1KM PROCENO (ELEV 419M, POP 573) 🏨 🏕 ⊚ (175.4KM)
Tradition says this ancient and picturesque hill town was founded in the 6th c. BC by the Etruscans. Its medieval fortress is now a posh hotel (www.castellodiproceno.it) and its most elegant building, the **Palazzo Sforza**, is town hall. (Bus: 6 times daily to Acquapendente, www.tiemmespa.it.)

⌂ **Ostello del Pellegrino** 🅾 🅳🅾 🆁 🅺 🆂 🆉 1/4, €10/-/-/-, Piazza della Libertà 23, rossiclaudio210@gmail.com, tel 339 258 6470 or 348 264 0781. Nearby restaurant with pilgrim menu €12.

⌂ **Parrocchia San Salvatore** 🅾 🅿🆃 🆁 🅺 🅱🆃 🅶🆃 🆆 🆂 5/5, €Donation, Piazza San Salvatore, tel 340 226 5595.

Continue downhill out of town and turn right off the main road onto a narrow asphalt road that leads to a steep path and ultimately back to the SR2 Via Cassia, where you find a fountain and rejoin the official track (**3.3km**) to turn uphill into **Acquapendente**.

Official route
At Ponte a Riga turn left onto the highway to cross the Rigo River and after the bridge fork left onto a gravel track near the roadway where you are safe from traffic. After a time this path returns to the highway and you walk alongside it again,

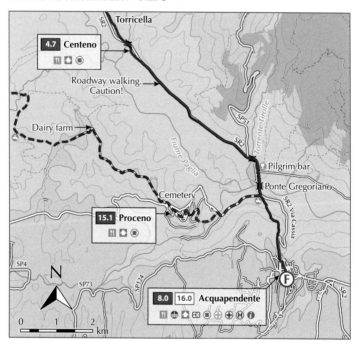

forking left onto the former Via Cassia roadway, here a broken asphalt surface that takes you through the settlement of **Torricella** (**3.5km**), returning to the new Via Cassia (SR2) having saved a couple hundred meters of highway walking. Cross the Torrente Elvella and then fork right to enter **Centeno**, the last safe place on the SR2 Via Cassia.

4.7KM CENTENO (ELEV 285M, POP 70) 🍴 🏠 ⦿ (177.7KM)

This tiny roadside village on the floor of the Paglia Valley at the Tuscany/Lazio border hosted its most famous visitor in 1633 when **Galileo** was quarantined here for nearly three weeks due to a plague in Tuscany while on his way to the Inquisition in Rome. La Dogana Ristorante (www.ladogana.eu) is closed Tues evening and Wed. (Bus: https://servizi.cotralspa.it, €1.1, 12:15, 15:55, 18:45. Taxi: call Morena Piazzai 335 785 1999.) Consult online resources for available hotels.

Now brace yourself for 6–7km of roadside ennui punctuated by a few moments of terror as large trucks and fast cars race along the highway within inches of you. Before a curve there is a fork right for a few hundred meters that keeps you off a dangerous stretch, and the **SP51** highway (**4.3km**) merges from the left just before you cross the **Torrente Tirolle**.

Continue along the highway, passing a pilgrim bar (**0.6km**) to the left and then crossing the 16th c. **Ponte Gregoriano** over the Paglia River. The Paglia here flows west to east from its headwaters at Monte Amiata, passing Acquapendente and, in 25km, Orvieto before joining the Tiber. Now turn right off the Via Cassia onto an asphalt road that begins here at the junction where the Proceno option rejoins (**0.7km**, fountain). Turn left immediately on a narrow asphalt road that climbs the forested ridge ahead, sometimes rather steeply. The road ends at the Via Cassia as it enters **Acquapendente**. Turn right, continuing uphill, then fork left into town and right at the signs, arriving in a few blocks in the central square, Piazza Fabrizio (**2.4km**).

8.0KM ACQUAPENDENTE (ELEV 383M, POP 5428)
🛏 ⊕ 🛄 🄲 ▣ ⊕ ⊕ 🄷 ❶ (169.7KM)

Archeological finds in the area show that Acquapendente was inhabited in pre-Roman times, though it is mentioned first in the 9th c. under the name 'Farisa.' By the 10th c. it had assumed the name Acquapendent (Latin: *Acquipendium*, tr: 'hanging waters'), most likely due to waterfalls along the Paglia River below town. The town grew up around the Via Francigena, with Rome-bound traffic entering near today's Monastery of Santa Chiara – once a tower among the fortifications – moving to the old city gathered around the Church of Santa Vittoria, and then toward the Basilica Cathedral on the far side of town, set below the imperial castle on the hill above. Its oft-rebuilt walls helped it fend off attacks from its principal rival, Orvieto, just down the Paglia River valley, and protected it during constant wars between imperial forces and those of the Papal States.

The most notable feature of this pleasant center is its **Basilica Cattedrale di San Sepolcro**, itself a site of pilgrimage due to the relics it contains of St Bernard of Castro, and more importantly the reputed drops of the blood of Christ on a stone brought from the Holy Sepulchre in Jerusalem. The church's low, plain exterior gives little hint of the treasure inside, but the beautifully preserved must-see 10th c. **crypt**, just below the main altar, casts an air of dark mystery to the relic shown there behind glass. Across the street the town's tourist information center is housed in a structure known as the 'Julia de Jacopo Tower.' Here in 1550 a courageous local girl closed the door in the city walls left open by soldiers defending the city, allowing it to withstand an attack by invaders.

Another important site is the **Museo della Città**, set in a 17th c. palazzo, which houses local artifacts and a museum of the Via Francigena.

⛺ **Associazione Casa di Lazzaro** 🔲 6/30, €Call, Via Cappuccini 23, accoglienza@casadilazzaro.org, tel 076 373 0177 or 339 432 7383.

⛺ **La Casa del Pellegrino** 🔲 🔲 🔲 🔲 4/13, €Donation, Via Roma 51, tel 347 166 2919. Unheated. Closed 1 Nov to 1st Sunday after Easter.

⛺ **La Casa di Adria** 🔲 🔲 🔲 🔲 🔲 🔲 2/3, €-/20/38/54, Via XXV Aprile, adriadionisi@gmail.com, tel 334 857 3734. Closed Oct–Mar. Reservation req.

The 10th c. crypt of Acquapendente's Cattedrale di San Sepolcro

SECTION 2: LAZIO

The first view of St Peter's Basilica as seen from Monte Mario Park

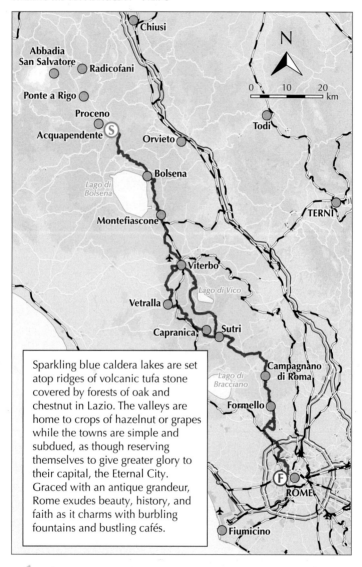

Sparkling blue caldera lakes are set atop ridges of volcanic tufa stone covered by forests of oak and chestnut in Lazio. The valleys are home to crops of hazelnut or grapes while the towns are simple and subdued, as though reserving themselves to give greater glory to their capital, the Eternal City. Graced with an antique grandeur, Rome exudes beauty, history, and faith as it charms with burbling fountains and bustling cafés.

STAGE 11
Acquapendente to Bolsena

Start	Acquapendente, Piazza Fabrizi
Finish	Bolsena, Piazza Santa Cristina
Distance	23.2km
Total ascent	503m
Total descent	564m
Difficulty	Moderate
Duration	6½hr
Percentage paved	23%
Hostels	Bolsena 23.2km

The stage has two distinct halves. The first is among flat fields of hay and grain with little shade and few distinguishing characteristics. After a low climb to San Lorenzo Nuovo and a first view of Lago di Bolsena, the rest of the day is spent in quiet forests, for a time on a serene forest path but otherwise on easy gravel roads with views to the lake. The stage ends at scenic, lakeside Bolsena with its historic castle and church. With ample food establishments, San Lorenzo Nuovo makes an excellent midday stop for refreshment.

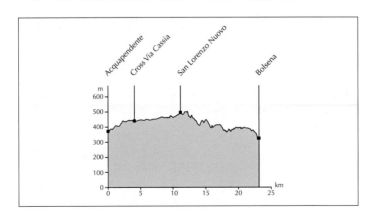

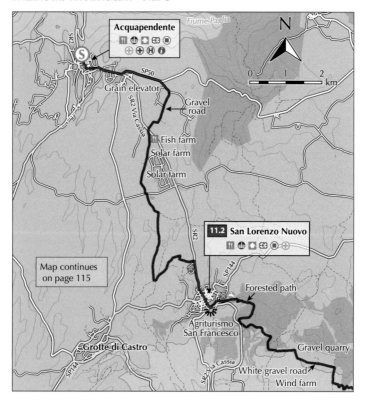

Looking into the face of the Fabrizi statue in the main piazza, go straight ahead to the end of the piazza and veer to your left, picking up the VF signs that aim you to the Civic Museum and the Basilica Cathedral, whose crypt is open early and is very much worth a visit. Continue past the cathedral on the sidewalk of the Via Cassia, passing supermarkets and suburban businesses, heading uphill under stately plane trees. Fork left in the direction of Torre Alfina on the SP50 (**1.2km**), noting the sign that announces the time to Bolsena as 5½hr. Walk alongside this road, first on an asphalt sidewalk and then on the road itself with views of a crenelated tower ahead as you share the road with cars and sometimes heavy trucks.

Atop the hill at a large **grain elevator** (**1.2km**) fork right onto a narrow asphalt road where the route steers you onto a wide, flat plateau of potato and grain

114

fields with low ridges in the distance on either side. Turn right onto a gravel road (**0.4km**) that leads into these fields. Cross the **SR2 Via Cassia** (**1.3km**), arriving at a **fish farm** that offers panini and snacks. Continue on this agrarian plateau past two **solar energy farms**, the back of some industrial estates on the Via Cassia, and to the right, more fields with mountains in the far distance. Eventually the fields end and you circumnavigate a low hill to find yourself once more at the Via Cassia (**6.0km**). Turn right, find a sidewalk on the right, pass an artistically modern pilgrim rest area at a sports field, then head up the hill and into town.

11.2KM SAN LORENZO NUOVO (ELEV 495M, POP 2109)
🏨 🚉 🏪 🏧 ⊙ ⊕ (158.5KM)

The original settlement at San Lorenzo alle Grotte (tr: 'San Lorenzo at the caves'), known since Etruscan times, sat along the shore of Lago di Bolsena along the Via Cassia, near caves set in the tall ridge. Due to the lack of trade along the route and the presence of malaria, the town and highway were relocated in 1774 to their present position on the tall bluff above, giving 'San Lorenzo Nuovo' (tr: 'New San Lorenzo') a new beginning, but forsaking the medieval and Renaissance buildings that would have made it a charming town today. A 12th c. **Byzantine cross** is one of the few items moved from the lower town and now stands in the 18th c. Church of San Lorenzo Martire. Potatoes – the primary local crop – are feted in mid-August each year when the Piazza Europa becomes an open-air restaurant during the Sagra degli Gnocchi festival. Consult online resources for available hotels.

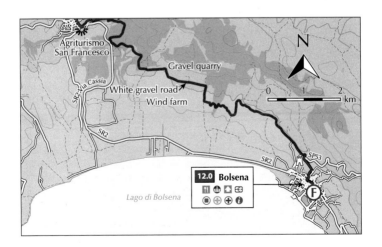

The Church of San Lorenzo Martire towers above Piazza Europa in San Lorenzo Nuovo

As you crown the hill in San Lorenzo a view opens ahead to **Lago di Bolsena**, which on a clear day you can see in its totality.

At 114km², **Lago di Bolsena** is Europe's largest volcanic lake. Between 100,000 and 200,000 years ago successive volcanic eruptions led to the collapse of the earth's crust in the volcano's caldera, forming the lake and its two islands. Underground springs and stormwater runoff fill the lake, which has an outlet to the sea through the Marta River.

Walk down to the overlook and then find the grassy path (**0.4km**) across the highway that heads left, behind homes near the end of the park. The route at first follows this path and then picks up asphalt lanes through a series of suburban neighborhoods, passing another artistic pilgrim rest area (fountain), and onto a very pleasant **forested path** (**0.4km**) of wildflowers and birdsong. The path at first traverses the hillside, then descends, and ultimately ends at a tree farm where you turn right to head downhill. Another right leads to a rough, two-track gravel road, ending at a wider gravel road just before the Via Cassia.

Quiet streets in the old town of Bolsena

Turn left here and begin the longest climb of the day, occasionally with wide views of the lake to the right. After a couple of summits and descents, the road turns to asphalt at the first vista where you can see a castle near the lakeshore – the first glimpse of Bolsena. Straight ahead now you can see a reddish-brown ridge where a quarry is slowly consuming the hillside. Turn right just before the **gravel quarry** (**4.1km**), heading downhill, once again with majestic views to the lake. The road veers left and makes a long, straight course through fields that slope toward the right, all with wide views of the lake. At the end of the largest field the road turns right, heads downhill briefly, and turns left before a wind farm.

Now the route follows a series of narrow gravel lanes heading uphill and down to keep you away from the Via Cassia traffic and tantalize you with views of the bejeweled lake. At one point an observant person in good weather can even spot the top of the dome and the fortress of Montefiascone above Bolsena ahead. The gravel diversions end at an asphalt road where you turn left at a switchback to merge onto the **SP53** (**6.3km**) that leads among stately trees right to the castle (**0.5km**) above town.

12.0KM BOLSENA (ELEV 323M, POP 3903) ▥ ⊕ ⌂ Ⓒ ◉ ⊕ ⊕ ❶ (146.3KM)

Sigeric lists the **Church of Santa Cristina** in this charming, lakeside town as his Stage VIII, but it wasn't until nearly 300 years later that the church's most famous event took place. In 1263, while a priest who doubted the concept of Transubstantiation was consecrating the host, the bread he was blessing suddenly began to drip blood onto his hands and the cloth below. In response, the following year Pope Urban IV created the Feast of Corpus Christi, now celebrated in Catholic churches throughout the world. The miracle, along with the relics of 3rd c. martyr Saint Cristina, which have been housed in the church for many centuries, made Bolsena a prime pilgrimage destination in its own right. In 1156 Pope Adrian IV ordered Bolsena to be fortified and a castle and walls were built around the village. In 1295 the Monaldeschi House of Orvieto overcame the city and improved the castle, now called **La Rocca Monaldeschi della Cervara**. It has been razed and reinforced many times over the centuries and currently houses a municipal museum. In good weather pilgrims may enjoy taking a dip in the very swimmable waters of **Lago di Bolsena**, a few blocks west of the town center. (Bus: to Montefiascone, 5 times daily, https://servizi.cotralspa.it.)

🏠 **Casa di Preghiera Santa Cristina** Ⓞ Ⓓⓞ Ⓡ Ⓚ Ⓦ Ⓢ Ⓩ 4/22, €-/-/-/-, Corso Cavour 70, tel 346 604 4158. In old city center.

🏠 **Suore del Santissimo Sacramento** Ⓞ Ⓓⓞ Ⓡ Ⓢ 4/18, €10/-/-/-, Piazza Santa Cristina 14, tel 076 158 6210. In old city center.

🏠 **Foresteria Santa Maria del Giglio** Ⓟⓣ Ⓡ Ⓦ Ⓢ 18/24, €Call, Via Madonna del Giglio 49, **www.monasterystays.com**, info@conventobolsena.org, tel 076 179 9066. On hillside above town. Indoor pool and large gardens.

Take narrow and steep cobblestone lanes down to the lowest level of the old city and find pleasant Piazza San Rocco. Turn left and follow the main pedestrian street through town to reach Piazza Santa Cristina, the stage end (**0.4km**).

Square turrets of La Rocca Monaldeschi della Cervara loom above Bolsena

STAGE 12
Bolsena to Montefiascone

Start	Bolsena, Piazza Santa Cristina
Finish	Montefiascone, Piazza Vittorio Emanuele
Distance	16.4km
Total ascent	638m
Total descent	356m
Difficulty	Moderate
Duration	5½hr
Percentage paved	34%
Hostels	Montefiascone 16.4km
Note	There are no services until Montefiascone, so bring a snack to give you energy partway through this short stage.

Until the last few busy and bleak kilometers into Montefiascione the stage is full of serenity and calm. Gravel roads and paths among fields and forests offer tranquility and occasionally a peaceful view of the lake, though it all comes at the price of a few steep climbs of 50–150m. Plan your visit to the Roca dei Papi overlook before dusk, since it doesn't open in the morning until 09:00, after many pilgrims have already departed.

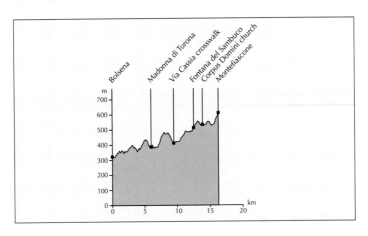

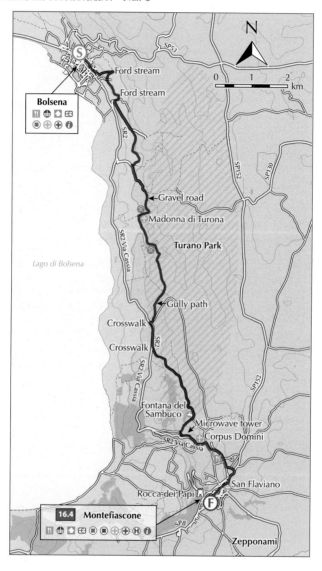

Bolsena

Ford stream
Ford stream

Lago di Bolsena

Gravel road
Madonna di Turona

Turano Park

Gully path

Crosswalk
Crosswalk

Fontana del Sambuco
Microwave tower
Corpus Domini
SR2 Via Cassia

San Flaviano

Rocca dei Papi
16.4 Montefiascone

Zepponami

Continue past Piazza Santa Cristina onto the pleasant and picturesque Corsaro Della Republica heading toward the Basilica of Santa Cristina. As you pass the church and head through the yellow Porta Romana, it seems at first you are headed toward the far green ridge, but instead the route takes you left just before the avenue of umbrella pines and snakes you through suburban streets before turning left just before a school. Here you begin to climb somewhat steeply on asphalt, veering right partway up onto a level dirt road where you **ford** a stream (**1.1km**) and then continue up on the other side.

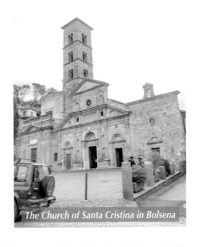

The Church of Santa Cristina in Bolsena

Soon you come to a gravel road that traverses the hillside with views to the right, climbing through vineyards. When the road ends at a house, continue to the left of the home and soon pick up a driveway that descends among olive trees. **Ford** a second stream (**0.9km**) and then take a gravel road that curves uphill to the right. Turn left when the road ends and immediately right onto an asphalt road which you follow straight as it turns to gravel and signs leads you right to pass through an olive orchard and into a wood (**1.4km**). Continue on an earthen path before turning right on a brown gravel road and passing a white gate. Turn left on a narrow asphalt road (**1.0km**) to begin another easy climb, this time on a forest drive. Fork right at a vineyard onto a **gravel road** and turn right just after a picnic area under oak trees. Continue to descend, entering the **Turano Park**.

> The **Turano Archeological and Naturalistic Park** rests among the hills of the Vulsini mountains, including the basins of the Turona and Arlena streams. The park shelters a diversity of plants and animals, as well as archeological sites from as early as the 9th c. BC. Artifacts from the digs are kept at the La Rocca Monaldeschi Museum back in Bolsena.

Turn left at the **Madonna di Turona chapel** (**1.8km**), going uphill on white gravel road at first, climbing and then descending through a forest of oak. Come alongside a low waterfall and then turn left to cross a stream on a wooden bridge. Pass a stone building and walk uphill on gravel, where after the steepest portion you emerge from the woods into a vineyard. Continue when you come to a summit at the vineyard with a picnic table on the right, then begin to descend as you see houses on the ridges ahead, a hint that civilization is nearby. On the most distant ridge you can now catch a glimpse of the dome of Montefiascone's Basilica of Santa Margherita.

Early evening at Piazza Vittore Emanuele in Montefiascone

Follow along as the road comes into a gathering of homes with large gardens behind stone walls, continuing to a large, gravel farm lot. From here head carefully downhill on a **gully-like path** (**2.8km**) of volcanic rock between two fields. The gully path ends at an asphalt road leading to the **SR2 Via Cassia Nord** (**0.6km**) where there is a button-activated **crosswalk**. Follow along on a roadside paths until in a few hundred meters the path ends as a second pushbutton **crosswalk** (**0.7km**) leads back across the highway onto a wide gravel road heading toward the ridge.

Continue through woods and olive groves as the road turns to asphalt at the first collection of houses. After a long and steady climb, interrupted by the **Fontana del Sambuco** (**2.4km**, water), turn right onto another asphalt road that heads up the ridge. Soon fork right onto a gravel road and continue to climb, aiming to the right of a tall microwave tower. At the summit (**0.7km**), arrive at an asphalt road with an astounding view of the valley leading down to the lake. Turn left and descend on asphalt with views ahead of the fortress and church dome of upper Montefiascone.

The road ends at the SR2 Via Cassia where you merge left onto an asphalt sidewalk, coming to the tall, squarish **Church of Corpus Domini** (**0.6km**) which sits above the road at the '100km to Rome' marker (perhaps true for cars, but the remaining distance for walkers on the VF is 132.8km). Veer left off the Via Cassia at a tall bank building and continue to climb on an arterial road devoid of all charm and, until the first café/bar (**0.8km**), devoid of services. Come to a wide intersection after a car dealership and turn left. The road now curves to the right, with the 15th c. Oratorio of Santa Maria della Grazie on the left. Fork left in a few hundred meters to come to the 11th c. **Church of San Flaviano** (**1.1km**), worth a visit for its frescoes, sculptures and Lombardian capitals if it is open.

Head uphill alongside the church, climbing the driveway steeply up to reach the SR2 Via Cassia and the city gate just beyond. Cross under the gate and continue steeply uphill, arriving at Piazza Vittore Emanuele (**0.5km**).

16.4KM MONTEFIASCONE (ELEV 602M, POP 13,520)
⊞ ⊕ ⊡ ⓒ ⊚ ⊙ ⊕ ⊕ ⊕ ❶ (130.0KM)

The first mention of Montefiascone in documents is in 853, though the Etruscan roots of the town suggest it is at least a millennium older. Its commanding position on the Via Francigena and proximity to Rome made it an important stronghold for the papacy, and it was besieged in 1093 by Emperor Henry IV. In the 13th and 14th c. it reached its zenith as a residence of popes and Papal legates but had already begun to decline by the 15th c., a process that was accelerated by the plague of 1657 and earthquake of 1697. The town was also damaged in two Allied bombings in May 1944. The 15th–17th c. **Basilica Cathedral of Santa Margherita** has one of the largest domes in Italy. It can be seen for many miles in all directions and contains the remains of the 4th c. martyr Santa Margherita of Antioch, one of the saints mentioned in the visions of Joan of Arc. It also holds relics of St Lucia Filippini, 17th–18th c., an educator of girls who established 52 schools.

The **San Flaviano Church**, passed on the way up to town, is the city's oldest and was visited by Sigeric as his Stage VII Sce Flaviane. In 1896 a series of frescoes were discovered hidden under paint and its elaborate columnar capitals hearken from the Lombard period. The church also includes the grave of Defuk, servant of a traveling bishop who sent him to scout ahead for the best white wines. He would write 'Est!' (tr: 'There is!') on the doorway of each inn whose wine was good enough. At one Montefiascone establishment he excitedly wrote 'Est! Est! Est!', which has since become an appellation for a particular local vintner, but also in general a proud description for all the local white varieties. Remains of the fortified Papal summer residence at the summit of town are preserved as the **Rocca dei Papi** park and pilgrim viewpoint which has an epic view over Lago di Bolsena. Museum and viewpoint open daily, 09:00–13:00, 15:30–18:30, €5. (Bus: https://servizi.cotralspa.it, 8 times daily to Viterbo. Train: connection to Viterbo from Zepponami station 2km away.)

⛪ **Convento Cappuccini** Pr Do R S 2/30, €12/20/-/-, Via San Francesco 2, edybertolo@libero.it, tel 347 590 0953. €5 linens.

⛪ **Domus Peregrini** Do R Br Dr S 1/20, €Donation, Via Paoletti 3, immacolatacorraggio1958@gmail.com, tel 338 183 8216 or 320 777 2586. 3km beyond town but on trail.

⛪ **Monastero San Pietro** Do R K Br W S 10/30, €Donation, Via Garibaldi 31, benedettineap.mf@gmail.com, tel 076 182 6066. Reservations req.

⛪ **Camere San Flaviano** O Pr R Br G S 4/15, €-/20/40/60, Via Cannelle 80, cameresanflaviano@gmail.com, tel 328 281 8278 or 338 126 7398.

STAGE 13

Montefiascone to Viterbo

Start	Montefiascone, Piazza Vittore Emanuele
Finish	Viterbo, Piazza del Plebiscito
Distance	18.1km
Total ascent	247m
Total descent	515m
Difficulty	Easy
Duration	4¾hr
Percentage paved	33%
Hostels	Viterbo 18.1km

A stage of contrasts: beautiful views, a peaceful descent to a rural valley, a free dip in thermal baths and a long walk among fields – and then a noisy and nerve-wracking walk among speeding cars and trucks up into the grimy side of workaday Viterbo. After making it into the old city, some exploration reveals the town's history and considerable charm. The only services between Montefiascone and the first businesses of Viterbo are at the hot springs, so if you're not stopping there, plan to bring a snack and ample water.

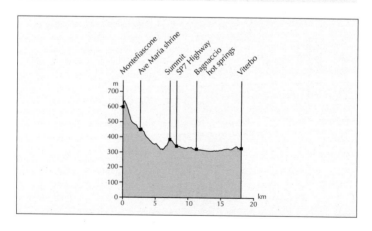

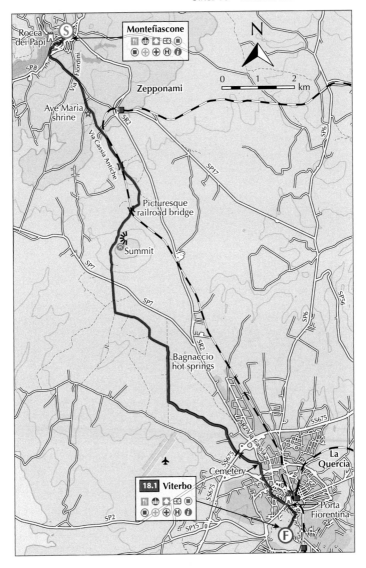

From Piazza Vittore Emanuele follow the signs uphill through a labyrinth of streets to the **Rocca dei Papi**. Though the Torre di Pellegrini and museum don't open until 09:00 the park still offers wide views over Lago di Bolsena. Find the stairway along the railing facing the lake and head down the ramp, through the parking lot and past the pilgrim monument with its own view over the lake. Walk toward the two-towered Church of San Bartolomeo, then go through a gate next to the church and turn left to continue downhill. At the stop sign cross the road and find the narrow concrete drive that will take you down a very steep hill. The road turns to gravel and enters the woods, coming out of the woods and turning to asphalt, all the time leading more or less straight down to the valley floor. Ahead you can see the Cimini mountains behind Viterbo, about 15km across the valley of fields and farms, which are the day's itinerary.

Go straight at the stop sign, crossing the **Via Fiordini** (1.7km) and continue straight ahead. Very soon turn right onto a two-track dirt path that descends through a narrow margin of trees separating the fields and orchards. The large, flat, rounded stones underfoot are part of an ancient Roman road. Fork left at an **Ave Maria shrine** (1.0km) and begin to walk on a longer stretch of Roman road, the **Via Cassia Antiche**.

> Named for Cassius Longinus, an important Roman official, the **Via Cassia** was built by the Romans in the 2nd c. BC to link Rome with Florence. Documents attest to its uniform width of 13 Roman feet (3.9m), and its engineering and construction techniques result in many stretches of the road being useable for foot and vehicular traffic to this day. Look for grooves worn by centuries of wagon wheels. The route of the Via Francigena continues roughly to follow the Via Cassia before turning onto the Via Trionfale just before Rome.

After climbing for a time, the road makes a shady and pleasant descent through trees among gated properties until it peters out to a dirt lane alongside railroad tracks, passing a sheep pasture as it heads downhill. Cross left under the railroad tracks (2.0km) onto a sometimes muddy road which comes to a low summit, descends, turns and then forks right to cross back to the other side of the tracks at a **picturesque railroad bridge** (1.4km) with serious mud issues in wet weather. After the bridge, fork right on the dirt road and head uphill, leaving the tracks behind and heading around the hill to the right of the tracks with views back to Montefiascone at a summit (picnic table).

Now the road descends, aiming at the highway on the valley floor. Cross the **SP7** (2.1km) and continue straight on the gravel road. Soon, vistas of Viterbo open before you again, nestled at the foot of the mountain. Follow the signs, wending among flat fields to reach the **hot springs** at Parco Terme Bagnaccio (3.0km, snack kiosk, www.bagnaccio.it, open daily until midnight), where pilgrims are welcome to relax free in the thermal springs gathered into cement-lined outdoor pools.

Continue on the gravel road as it turns left before the airport, and after a good long time come alongside large properties of big-box retail stores on the left. Cross under the **SS675** highway and come to a very large and modern **cemetery (4.2km)** on the right. Just afterward is the modern **Via Cassia** where you turn right, following signs that lead through a bleak panoply of suburban auto businesses interspersed with tall, concrete retaining walls among the entrails of this city. Finally arrive at the **Porta Fiorentina (1.8km)** where you head straight downhill on cobblestones to the end of Via Matteotti. Turn right to walk along the Corso Italia, the bustling, main pedestrian street that spills into the Piazza Plebiscito at stage end (**0.8km**).

18.1KM VITERBO (ELEV 334M, POP 67,804)
🍴 ⊕ 🛏 🅲 ◉ ⊕ ⊕ 🅷 𝒊 (111.9KM)

The gritty entry into Viterbo can give the wrong impression of this otherwise charming and historic city, whose existence dates to an era long before Rome. Viterbo is center of the Tuscia region of Etruscan culture (9th–4th c. BC), whose vestiges and influences are still quite visible. As a stop on the Via Cassia, the city held a strategic role in Roman times, but it grew to prominence in the Middle

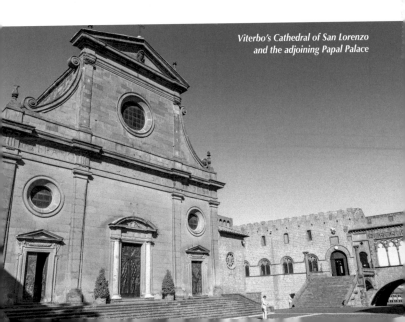

Viterbo's Cathedral of San Lorenzo and the adjoining Papal Palace

Ages as a stop on the Via Francigena. Sigeric's Stage VI Sce Valentino overnight was at the hot springs of Bullicame near Viterbo airport at the entrance to town. As an outer defense of the Papal States, Viterbo was heavily fortified against invasion, and its walls are intact and visible today. In the 12th and 13th c. the town was a favored safe place for popes, and Pope Eugenius III was besieged behind these walls in the 12th c. The presence of the Papacy made it one of the most prominent cities of central Italy, with a population of over 60,000. Wars and rebellions in the 14th c. caused popes to avoid the town and it declined to become a mere regional capital within the Papal States.

Viterbo's architectural treasures are found beyond its commercial zone at the **Piazza Duomo**, where the bare but beautiful 12th c. Romanesque **Cathedral of San Lorenzo** can be found, along with the **Palazzo dei Papi**, Papal seat for 24 years (1257–1281), whose lace-like loggia is visible just to the right of the cathedral. Less grand is the tiny 11th c. **Church of San Silvestro**, built on what was once the main market square. Viterbo has a stock of Romanesque churches, including **Santa Maria Nuova**, **San Sisto**, and **San Giovanni in Zoccoli**. Santa Rosa is remembered in a 19th c. church that bears her name. Several civic buildings surround the **Piazza del Plebescito**, including the 15th c. **Palazzo Comunale**. Worth a tour is the **Museo Civico**, which houses Roman and Etruscan finds as well as Renaissance-era paintings. Tourists come to enjoy the city, but many also spend time at the famous hot springs located nearby at **Terme dei Papi, Bullicame, Carletti, and Masse di San Sisto** (see www.termediviterbo.it).

⌂ Convento Cappuccini 🄾 🄿🅣 🄳🄾 🅁 🅂 2/14, €12/-/15/-, Via San Crispino 6, edy-bertolo@libero.it, tel 347 590 0953 or 076 122 0761. €5 linens. Arrive before 20:00.

⌂ Ospitale dei Pellegrini 🄳🄾 🅁 🄱🅯 🅂 ?3/14, €12/-/-/-, Via San Pellegrino 49, ospi-taledelpellegrino@gmail.com, mirvin@virgilio.it, tel 334 696 0175.

⌂ Parrocchia San Leonardo Murialdo 🄿🅣 🄳🄾 🅁 🄺 🄱🅯 🄳🅯 🅆 🅂 🅭 6/20, €10/-/-/-, Via Caduti IX Stormo, snc, angelobissoni@gmail.com, tel 348 291 0500 or 076 122 0488. Open Jul–Sept 10.

⌂ B&B Casa di Ale 🄾 🄿🅣 🅁 🄺 🄱🅯 🅂 2/6, €-/15/-/-, Via Monte Cervino 13, alessan-dra.croci222@gmail.com, tel 320 011 2384. €5 breakfast available.

Viterbo

1. Cattedrale di San Lorenzo
2. San Silvestro
3. Santa Maria Nuova
4. San Sisto
5. San Giovanni in Zoccoli
6. Santuario di Santa Rosa
7. Basilica di San Francesco all Rocca

A. Ospitale dei Pellegrini
B. to Parrocchia San Leonardo Murialdo
C. to Convento Cappuccini

1. Museo Civico
2. Museo Nazionale Etrusco Rocca Albornoz

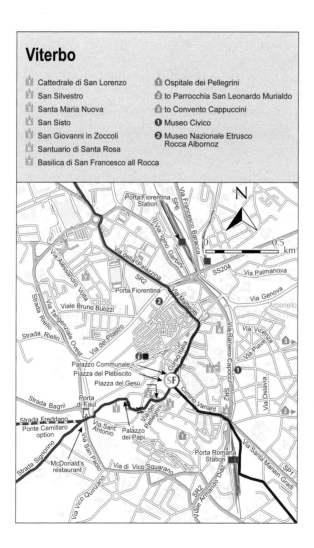

ALTERNATIVE STAGE 14/15
Cimino Variant: Viterbo to Sutri

Start	Viterbo, Piazza del Plebescito
Finish	Sutri, Piazza Cavour
Total distance	31.3km
Total ascent	940m
Total descent	972m
Difficulty	Hard
Duration	9hr
Percentage paved	60%
Accommodation	San Martino al Cimino, 8.7km, Ronciglione 24.9km, Sutri, 31.3km
Note	For map see Stages 14 and 15

Rather than the official route of 41km, usually covered in two days, a shorter but much more taxing option between Viterbo and Sutri is the historic Via Cimina that shortcuts over Monte Fogliano of the Cimini Mountains along trails and quiet roads through the Lago di Vico Nature Reserve to Sutri in just 31.3km over a single day. Though this unofficial variant is quicker to Sutri, its stiff uphill climb makes it harder and it does miss many of the Etruscan highlights of the Tuscia region available on the official route (www.variantecimimadellafrancigena.it).

If you choose this variant, begin at the Piazza Plebiscito in Viterbo and head uphill on the Via Garibaldi and follow 'Cimino Variant' signs toward San Martino al Cimino. This stage includes an option through historic **San Martino al Cimino** (turn-off at **7.7km**, additional 1km to town; food, accommodation). Afterward you have a choice of walking on the west side of the **Lago di Vico** (as shown) or the east. Either involves a taxing climb/descent up and down the chestnut, beech and oak covered mountain, with the west route climbing **Monte Fogliano** and enjoying views over **Punta del Lago di Vico** on the lake's south side. The route continues through **Poggio Cavaliere** (**22.2km**), **Ronciglione** (**2.6km**, food, groceries, bank, pharmacy, accommodation) and **Colle Diana** (**4.1km**, restaurant) before entering **Sutri** from the northwest. Arrive in Sutri on Via Garibaldi into Piazza Cavour (**2.4km**).

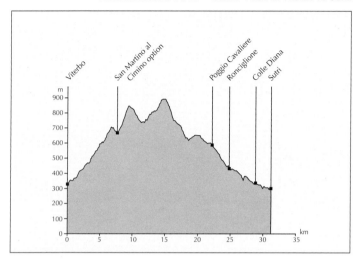

The neo-classical city gate of San Martino al Cimino

STAGE 14
Viterbo to Vetralla

Start	Viterbo, Piazza del Plebiscito
Finish	Vetralla, Piazza Umberto
Total distance	16.8km
Total ascent	340m
Total descent	363m
Difficulty	Easy
Duration	4½hr
Percentage paved	49%
Accommodation	Vetralla 16.8km

An easy and short day of walking among Etruscan 'Vie Cave' roads, olive orchards and sheep pastures. Viterbo's beautiful cathedral piazza begins the stage, while quiet Vetralla offers a convenient overnight.

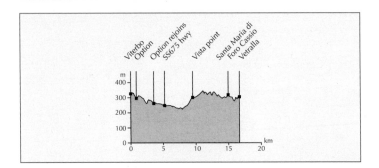

In the Piazza Plebiscito look toward the pink Prefettura government building and head along its left side, walking down the Via San Lorenzo with its shops, bars and restaurants. Turn right into Piazza Gesu and then veer left of the church to walk along the block-long Via dei Pellegrini, the historic pilgrim exit to Rome. Turn left to return to the Via San Lorenzo, crossing a bridge over the Via Sant'Antonio. Pass the Palazzo Farnese, and then come to Piazza Duomo, with the cathedral and its mismatched tower side-by-side. Go under the lace-like arches of the Palazzo dei Papi

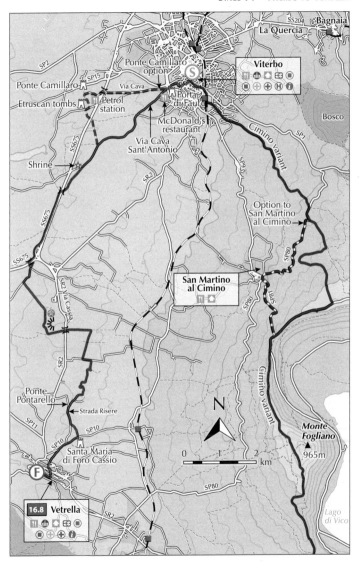

to the right, finding a stairway that leads down to Via San Clemente. Turn left here and head down the hill, out the **Porta di Faul** (**0.8km**) and cross the road toward the **McDonald's restaurant**. On the right side of the restaurant find yourself at an option. The main route forks left along the Strada Signorino, making its way through the steep walls of the **Via Cava Sant'Antonio**.

The mysterious, **Etruscan Vie Cave** (tr: 'excavated roads') in this region have provoked scholarly debate for centuries. They consist of narrow roadways cut like gashes into the soft, tufa stone over 2500 years ago. They usually lead from Etruscan settlements to nearby necropoli. Scholars suggest they were either cut through hillsides as part of an unknown funeral observance or because the iron-clad wheels of wagons made deep depressions in the soft tufa, necessitating the ongoing re-flattening of the roads. The Via Cava of Sant'Antonio runs to a depth of 12m, but in other locations, particularly near Pitigliano, they can be nearly twice as deep.

Cliff-like walls of an ancient via cava *frame a modern road near Viterbo (photo: Frank Müller)*

134

Ponte Camillaro option

An option forks right, heading through a separate via cava to visit Roman and Etruscan ruins, adding 1.3km to the day's total. Follow the road through the via cava, cross the **SS675** highway at a petrol station/pizzeria, turn right at the shrine to the martyrs Saints Valentino and Ilario, and walk about 150m to see the Roman bridge, originally part of the Via Cassia. Afterward follow signs to a series of covered and usually locked **Etruscan tombs** set in a field. The option crosses back under the highway and shortly afterward rejoins the main route.

Before the main route comes to the SS675 highway the option rejoins (**2.6km**). Follow signs to cross a small valley. When the asphalt road forks right at a **shrine** go straight ahead on a gravel road which becomes a dirt path and soon crosses under the SS675 highway (**1.8km**). Turn left on a gravel road that follows alongside the road before crossing under it again (**2.2km**), briefly circling back, and forking right to leave the highway. The gravel road soon turns to asphalt and begins to climb the hill just ahead. Partway up the hill, turn left onto a two-track dirt road leading gradually uphill between fields. Continue to climb among olive orchards on this very heavily rutted road of black sand. Come to a picnic table and a tall farmhouse ruin at the top of the hill and a view point (**2.2km**).

To the right you can see the vast, seaside **Maremma plain**, with flat farmland spreading into the distance until low mountains rise on the horizon. The area was once home to the *butteri* mounted cattle herders, and local livestock owners bred the large white Maremmano livestock dogs found throughout Italy, who take their name from this region.

Where the black sand road ends turn left on a white gravel road. From here, on a clear day, you can look toward the far ridge and see Montefiascone.The gravel road ends when you cross an asphalt road and then a bridge over the **Via Cassia** (**0.8km**). On the opposite side of the bridge continue uphill on asphalt where you can now see that some low ridges lie ahead. Partway up the hill turn right on a gravel road and descend on a series of paths and roads among olive orchards and sheep pastures where for the first time you see Vetralla to the left.

The paths and roads ultimately lead toward pavement at **Ponte Pontarello** (**3.7km**) on the asphalt **Strada Risere**, where you turn left. Watch for a left turn onto a grassy path that helps avoid some dangerous curves on this road as it comes closer to town. The road becomes a gravel drive among large houses and gardens and then ends at the **SP10** asphalt road (**1.0km**) where you turn right, using the sidewalk on the left side. Just to the left are the diminutive ruins of Santa Maria di Foro Cassio, all that is left of the original location of Vetralla, which was moved for defensive purposes in the Middle Ages to the ridge beyond. This location is listed as Sigeric's Stage V Furcari.

Soon fork left and descend to the valley floor, crossing a stream and heading uphill to the entrance to **Vetralla**, perched on towering Monte Fogliano above. Go straight ahead at the tall bulkhead at the top of this road and then arrive at the SR2 Via Cassia (**1.4km**). Cross the road and continue up the hill to come to the pedestrian Via Roma, turning right to find first the main piazza and then the church and Municipio at Piazza Umberto at stage end (**0.4km**).

Interior of Vetralla's Neo-classical Duomo

The 18th c Comune building in Vetralla shares a small piazza with the town's cathedral

16.8KM VETRALLA (ELEV 312M, POP 13,978)

⛺ ⊕ 🏠 🄴 ⓜ ⓜ ⊕ ⊕ ❶ (95.1KM)

The chaos in Rome had grown to such an extent that at his election in 1145, Pope Eugenius III was unable to reside in the city. He chose his headquarters from among local fortresses, landing on Vetralla for part of his reign. It was from here he announced the Second Crusade later that same year. Vetralla has been part of the Papal territories since the 8th c., except for a brief period when it was ruled by Viterbo.

Though well preserved, today's sleepy town is divided between a few businesses scattered along the Via Roma in the upper city and others along the busy Via Cassia highway a few meters below. Its most important architectural monument is the 12th c. **Church of San Francesco** with vividly decorated capitals in its nave and crypt and intricate, inlaid geometric floor tiles. The Duomo and the Comune building are both 17th and 18th c. creations, squeezed across from each other on a small piazza. Today's Vetralla is known regionally for its **living Nativity** observed with a 19th c. theme. (Train: station 3km SE at Botte, www. trenitalia.com. Bus: every 30min to Capranica, https://servizi.cotralspa.it.)

🛏 FamilARCA 🄾 ⓟ ⓓ ⓡ ⓚ ⓦ ⓢ ⓩ 2/13, €10/15/-/-, Via Cassia Botte 89, familarca@gmail.com, tel 334 786 8102, 339 352 0365. 1-week notice req to reserve.

🛏 Monastero Regina Pacis 🄾 ⓟ ⓡ ⓚ ⓑ ⓓ ⓦ ⓢ 22/44, €-/12/-/-, Via del Giardino 4, accoglienza@casareginapacis.com, tel 076 148 1519. Linens €3. Arrive 09:00–14:00 or 16:00–18:00.

STAGE 15
Vetralla to Sutri

Start	Vetralla, Piazza Umberto
Finish	Sutri, Piazza del Comune
Total distance	24.0km
Total ascent	475m
Total descent	511m
Difficulty	Moderate
Duration	6½hr
Percentage paved	29%
Accommodation	Capranica 16.4km, Sutri 24.0km

A leafy, easy and pleasant stage with forests and hazelnut orchards as bookends and delightful Capranica in the middle. Central Sutri is calm and lovely, with café-sitting in a classic Italian piazza the favored pastime. The ancient Etruscan sites at the base of town are some of the best in Italy.

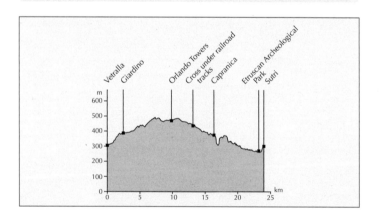

Walking down the aptly named Via Roma, fork left across from the peach-colored elementary school onto the Via San Michele. Coming to the **SR2 Via Cassia**, cross it by the pedestrian tunnel and continue uphill on the asphalt road

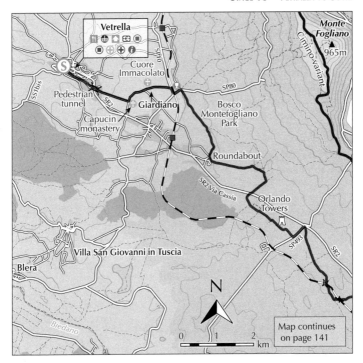

until it ends at the **Capuchin monastery** (**1.7km**), where you turn left. The road curves right, passing the **Cuore Immacolato di Maria church** (water fountain) as you enter the village of **Giardino** (**1.1km**).

When the road ends at the **SP10** highway turn right, walking for a couple of hundred meters before turning left at a bar and crossing the railroad tracks (**0.6km**). Continue on an asphalt road toward the low, wooded ridge ahead and turn right into a parking lot to pick up a mountain bike path that travels through the oak forest of the **Bosco Montefogliano Park**. Stay on this lovely trail under trees for about the next 4km, interrupted in the middle by a meadow and a brief walk across a **roundabout**. Continue to climb through woods, watching for a right fork that takes you downhill, emerging from the forest at an orchard.

Turn right onto a gravel road and descend to cross the Via Cassia (**4.9km**). Fork left after 50m to pick up a dirt road on the other side, very carefully watching the signs as the route cuts through hazelnut orchards, sometimes following

139

between rows of trees rather than a proper road or path. Coming to a fence in the orchard, follow its perimeter around to the left before going left at a white gravel road to continue through the orchards on a grassy drive. After a time come to a dirt orchard road and turn left as the road curves up a small hill, arriving at **Orlando Towers** (**1.5km**).

> Legends say that these three **towers** were built by Orlando (Italian for 'Roland'), a favorite general of Charlemagne and subject of the epic 11th c. poem *The Song of Roland*. In fact, historians suggest two of the towers are funeral monuments from the Roman period and the other is the remains of a bell tower from the 10th c. Church of Sancta Maria in Campis.

Continue through the orchard in the same direction and come in **500m** to an asphalt road, the **SP493**. Turn left here and follow it until just before the Via Cassia where you turn right onto an asphalt road, which soon turns to a well-graded gravel thoroughfare among woods and hazelnut orchards, with tall umbrella pines overhead at intervals. The road cuts a wandering path among orchards, crosses railroad tracks and continues, then suddenly turns left to descend under railroad tracks again (**3.3km**) and cross a small, seasonal creek on a modest bridge. Come to a summit, and then descend again. A road joins from the right and you soon cross under a single arched road bridge (**1.6km**) as you enter town. Fork left and follow this road up into the outskirts of town as it merges with an arterial road and then with the familiar SR2 Via Cassia. Come to the first city gate and then a second to find yourself in the heart of **Capranica** (**1.6km**).

16.4KM CAPRANICA (ELEV 371M, POP 5871)
🏨 ⊕ 🛏 🄲 🅢 🅜 ⊕ ⊕ 🛈 (78.7KM)

According to legends, goatherds from a nearby village fled Lombard invaders in the 8th c. and settled on a tufa hill for safety, calling their new village 'Capranica' (*capra* is 'goat' in Italian). However it was founded, the resulting town's Castrovecchio neighborhood is a delightful step back in time, with narrow streets and medieval architecture. The oldest building is the modest 9th c. **Church of San Pietro**, with its 14th c. frescoes of San Sebastian. The 13th–16th c. Church of San Francesco holds 15th c. frescoes in Renaissance style, while the **Church of San Giovanni** retains a dome from the 16th c. and a bell tower from the 1200s. The town may be even more notable for who passed through its gates. Charlemagne is documented to have passed through here in 800, the poet Petrarch in 1335 and Giuseppe Mazzini, the Italian patriot, about 500 years after that. From the Middle Ages to the Renaissance the town was part of the fiefdom of the powerful Anguillara family, whose name is remembered on the main pedestrian street in the old town. (Rome is accessible by train in 90min from the Capranica-Sutri station 3.5km from town, www.trenitalia.com.)

⌂ Casa San Pietro ⊙ ℝ 𝕂 Br 𝕎 𝕊 2/4, €-/20/40/60, Via Castelvecchio 54, alloggiosanpietro@gmail.com, tel 329 612 3945 or 389 312 2518.

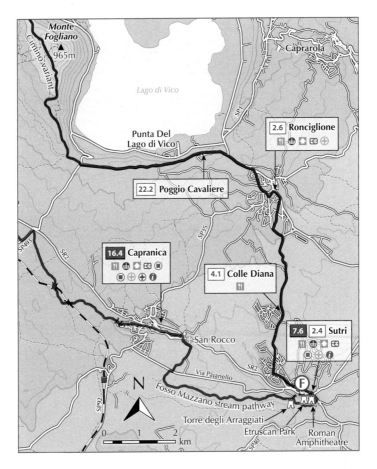

Pilgrims entering Capranica in the shade through the Porta del Ponte dell'Orologio

Continue along the Via degli Anguillara until it becomes a winding stairway that takes you down to the valley floor. Fork right toward the **Church of San Rocco**, and then left on a road behind it that climbs steeply up the hill. At the top, fork right and reach a summit among hazelnut trees, just afterward forking to the right again to descend on a wide, dirt path. The path ends at the **Via Pajanello** asphalt road where you go right 50m later onto a two-track gravel road leading downhill into the woods. Turn left to follow a pleasant and shaded path for 2km alongside the **Fosso Mazzano** stream (**2.3km**).

After a horse pasture the path becomes the driveway of a farmhouse and soon the first buildings of Sutri come into view ahead through the vegetation. At a gravel road T-junction, signs point you to the right onto a path alongside the **Etruscan Archeological Park** (**4.0**), one of the finest Etruscan sites in Italy. Behind and to the right is the 'Torre degli Arraggiati' or 'Torre San Paolo,' once part of a monastery complex which may have hosted Sigeric when he stayed at Sutri on Stage IV of his journey. A kiosk at the junction provides a detailed map of the park. A left turn takes you to the Via Cassia, the park's information center and an unmarked shortcut across the highway through the Via Porta Vecchia up into Sutri itself. A right turn takes you alongside the park's main sites and eventually across the SR2 highway (**0.9km**) where you can head left and up the hill to enjoy enchanting **Sutri**, finding its quiet, pedestrian square in the upper town (**0.5km**).

7.6KM SUTRI (ELEV 303M, POP 6624) 🏨 ⊕ 🛏 🅲 ◉ ⊕ 𝐢 (71.1KM)

Sutri's Piazza del Commune is as charming as any town square on the Via Francigena, but the town's history is far older than most. The Antichimissa Città di Sutri is a must-see, including the Etruscan necropolis, Roman amphitheater and frescoes of the Mitreo Tomb (€5, www.parchilazio.it/sutri/). As a border town between Rome and Etruria, Sutri is described in documents as the location of important Roman/Etruscan battles in the 4th and 3rd c. BC. **Ancient Etruscan tombs** carved in the soft tufa stone peek out from the low cliffs near the 1st c. BC **Roman amphitheater**, cut directly into the stone. Between the 5th and 8th c. AD Sutri played a role in conflicts between the Byzantines and Lombards, and in the 9th c. Charlemagne stayed here on his way to his coronation as Holy Roman Emperor. Legends say his sister, Berta, gave birth here in a cave to Orlando (Roland) who would become Charlemagne's beloved friend and trusted general. Pope Clement II was elected pope here at a conclave in 1046.

Sutri suffered a long, slow decline as its strategic importance waned. In 1878 a trove of jewelry, likely possessions of a 6th–7th c. Lombard queen or princess, was found near the town. The elaborate gold and precious stones of the Sutri Treasure are housed today in the British Museum. The medieval town is clustered atop the ridge of tufa stone, where the Romanesque structure of the **Church of San Silvestro** heads the list of historic buildings. The 13th c. Church of San Francesco was founded by the saint himself in 1222, but the building was damaged in WWII and has only recently been restored. While many older elements of the 13th c. **Co-cathedral of Santa Maria Assunta** (meaning it shares a bishop with other cathedrals) have been hidden by albeit lovely Baroque renovations or removed, its Cosmatesque (mosaic-like) floor survives along with its Romanesque crypt.

🏠 **Casa del Pellegrino** Ⓞ P̄r D̄o R̄ K̄ W̄ S̄ 2/7, €30/30/-/-, Via dei Saturnali 10, casadelpellegrino10@gmail.com, tel 338 418 1886 or 333 344 7870.

🏠 **Platea Cavour** Ⓞ P̄r R̄ K̄ B̄r W̄ S̄ 2/3, €-/20/40/-, Piazza Cavour 12, plateacavour@gmail.com, tel 329 213 6615.

🏠 **Casa Vacanze Salza** Ⓞ P̄r R̄ K̄ B̄r W̄ S̄ 3/6, €18/36/36/54, Via Ronciglione 38, diana.salza@gmail.com, tel 338 860 1088.

🏠 **Il Casaletto Salza** Ⓞ D̄o R̄ K̄ B̄r W̄ S̄ 3/4, €18/36/36/54, Via Martiri di Via Fani 14, casalettosalza@gmail.com, tel 338 860 1088. 20% winter surcharge for heating.

🏠 **Il Ritrovo degli Amici** Ⓞ P̄r R̄ K̄ B̄r W̄ 2/5, €20/-/40/-, Piazza della Rocca 2, francescoserrenti@gmail.com, tel 380 140 4330 or 327 702 6023.

Sutri's Etruscan and Roman-era tombs were carved into the soft, volcanic tufa stone

STAGE 16
Sutri to Campagnano di Roma

Start	Sutri, Piazza del Comune
Finish	Campagnano di Roma, Piazza Cesare Leonelli
Total distance	27.7km (3.2km shorter on the official route)
Total ascent	513m
Total descent	538m
Difficulty	Moderate
Duration	7½hr
Percentage paved	53%
Accommodation	Monterosi 13.0km, Campagnano di Roma 27.7km

With good weather this is an ideal walking day. The path is mostly among fields and in forests – far from traffic if you choose the quieter option after Sutri, although it adds 3.2km to the day. Monte Gelato, with its refreshing waterfalls, and Monterossi, with its shops and stores, give options for rest and supplies partway through the stage. Campagnano di Roma is a small town typical of Lazio, full of life in the evenings, particularly in the more modern piazza just outside the Porta Romana city gates.

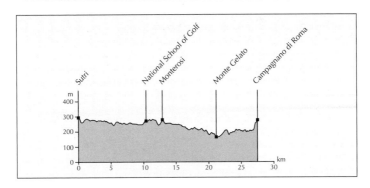

Head back downhill from Piazza del Commune on Via XXIV Maggio toward the Roman amphitheater at the bottom of the hill and then briefly walk on the gravel pedestrian sidewalk alongside the **Via Cassia**. Just after the amphitheater is

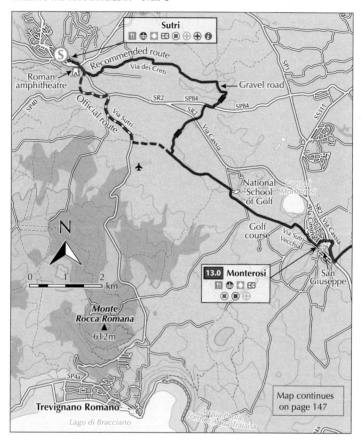

a pleasanter option, 3.2km longer but safer, that heads left on a detour through hazelnut orchards and pastures before bringing you back to the SP84 before reconnecting with the main route. The shorter, but more auto-oriented official route turns right just after the **Roman amphitheater**, following a path that leads to the narrow **SP40** asphalt road where you turn left. Arriving at the **SR2 Via Cassia** turn right and follow it briefly to a busy Y-junction where you turn right in the direction of Bracciano, to follow the narrow and busy **Via Sutri** until forking left where it joins the quieter and safer optional route.

Recommended option

To follow the safer option after the amphitheater, turn left on the asphalt **Via dei Creti** that leads up a small hill among tall shrubs and large, gated properties. After a summit, follow this road generally downhill for around 4km as it turns to gravel among hazelnut orchards and pastures, until the route turns right at a gravel road (**4.9km**), descending to a stream and then climbing again before ending at an asphalt road, the **SP84** (**1.0km**). Turn right and follow the roadside pathway for 100m before turning left on a white gravel road among factory-like warehouses separated by hayfields. Come now to the Via Cassia again (**0.7km**), which you carefully cross, heading straight across fields and then curving to the left. Descend slightly to cross a noisy creek on a small bridge and continue among the flat fields, aiming toward a tall, wooded ridge beyond. An **airfield** is just to the right. When the road ends, turn left and rejoin the main route, aiming down the valley to follow the rough trajectory of the Via Cassia.

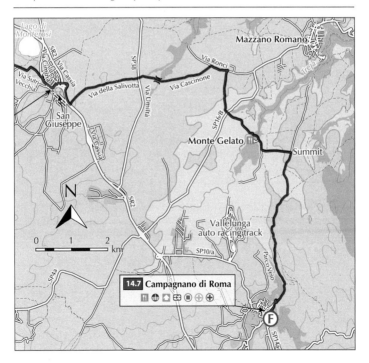

This road ends at an asphalt road with a golf course across the street. Turn right to climb a low hill and pass the entrance to the **National School of Golf** (**3.7km**). Just afterward the asphalt road turns right but the route continues straight onto a gravel road, passing the golf fairways and descending slightly as you catch glimpses of the homes and buildings of the next town. As the road enters **Monterosi** it veers to the left on the **Via Sutri Vecchia** and then merges with the busier **Via Cimina** before climbing the hill into town (**2.6km**).

13.0KM MONTEROSI (ELEV 280M, POP 4657) ⓘ ⊕ ⓐ Ⓒ ⓜ ⓜ ⊕ (58.1KM)

In its long history Monterosi's position on the Via Cassia spurred its prosperity, but also put it in the path of invaders like the Goths and Lombards aiming at the riches of Rome. Here Pope Hadrian IV met Federico Barbarossa in 1155 to crown him Holy Roman Emperor and here in 1649 Pope Innocent X's emissary, Monsignor Giarda, was assassinated on his way to make peace with the Duchy of Castro, which the pontiff would later destroy. In 1798 the Neapolitan Army was defeated here by the French as part of the Battle of Civita Castellana in the Second Coalition War. Nazi forces mined the approaches to Monterosi before Allied troops cleared the town in June 1944. The small, 30-hectare, volcanic **Lago Monterosi** sits within the city limits. Most visible to pilgrims is the unusual Renaissance-era **Chapel of San Giuseppe** with its dome standing atop its squared, Greek-cross nave. Consult online resources for available hotels.

Follow Via XIII Settembre through town until just before the central plaza and domed **Chapel of San Giuseppe** where you turn left and continue downhill. Walk alongside the SR2 Via Cassia, now a limited access highway, following the cloverleaf off-ramps as the sidewalk becomes a gravel path along the highway itself. After walking along the busy road for a brief time, turn left onto the gravel **Via della Sallivota** (**1.3km**) heading straight and flat across fields. Cross the **SP38 Via Umiltà** then continue on the gravel **Via Cascinone** on the opposite side as the road continues descending almost imperceptibly.

Cross a seasonal creek and come alongside large sheep pastures. The gravel road finally ends and you turn right on the asphalt **Via Ronci** (**4.3km**), going slowly uphill through a forest of oak trees, widely dispersed with little undergrowth. After the oak forest the road curves sharply right, with wide pastureland on the left. Cross the **SP16B** (**1.6km**) and continue straight on, climbing gradually at first. As you descend come to a large outdoor picnic area near the lovely and popular waterfall park of **Monte Gelato** (**1.1km**, restaurants).

A deserted farmhouse stands among sheep pastures after Monterosi

These diminutive, but picturesque **waterfalls** make a charming rest stop after Monterosi, though Monte Gelato can be busy with Roman families relaxing here on holiday weekends. In this public park the waters of the Treja River cascade down volcanic stone banks in the midst of what once was a mill complex and even before was an ancient settlement, with ruins nearby of a Roman villa. The park has a restaurant with picnic area and a more traditional restaurant just outside the gates (www.parchilazio.it/valledeltreja).

Fork left after the park to stay on the wider asphalt road as it climbs. The road ends at the summit, where you turn right to descend and climb again, the road turning to gravel as it nears houses. In about 10min the road ends and you turn right, climbing gradually toward some young hazelnut orchards. After passing a large barn the road veers off to the right, heading toward the Vallelunga motor racing track – just 1km to the right – while the VF route instead goes straight onto a narrower gravel road. Descend gradually at first, then more steeply as you continue through woods, crossing the bed of a seasonal stream and running alongside the **Parco Regionale di Veio** (see Stage 17).

Climb up the other side of the valley among pastures and small woods until the road ends at the wide curve of another gravel road. Turn right, cross a bridge and head onto a two-track gravel road that slowly climbs toward the steep green ridge with a tall spire surmounted by a bell-shaped cupola. Climb the ridge on switchbacks and fork left at the top as you come first to the San Giovanni Battista Church and then soon after to the Leonelli Piazza at the historic center of **Campagnano di Roma** (6.4km).

Campagnano di Roma's red town hall sits on the Piazza Leonelli at the heart of the village

14.7KM CAMPAGNANO DI ROMA (ELEV 280M, POP 11,586)
🍴 ⊕ 🛏 🄲 ◉ ⊕ ⊕ (43.4KM)

The medieval quarter of this ancient town has its charms, but in the evenings the center of activity is the **Parco Pubblico** just outside the Porta Romana. Originally called Baccano for a temple to Bacchus located on its summit, the town was wrested from the Etruscans by Rome in 241 BC. Sigeric identifies it as Stage III Bacane. By the 13th c. wealthy Romans were seeking refuge in the rural environs here (*campagna* tr: 'countryside') to avoid intermittent plagues and the town name was changed from its former, pagan appellation. Campagnano reached its prominence in the 15th–18th c. when the powerful Roman Orsini family maintained a castle here. Some houses from the 11th and 12th c. remain, while the 11th c. **Church of the Pietà**, which houses an important fresco, is the oldest public building. The unusual 15th c. **Gonfalone Church** has a central tower topped by a wrought-iron balustrade and sits on the sadly car-choked Piazza Leonelli, which is below the striking, red, 19th c. town hall. In between is the late Renaissance **Fontana Delfini**. (Bus: to La Storta 3 times daily, https://servizi.cotralspa.it.)

🛏 **Ostello Campagnano** Ⓞ Pr Do R K Br S 6/20, €20/35/40/75, Via di Sant'Andrea 65, info@ostellocampagnano.it, tel 331 600 4982. Near where you arrive into town, in the historic center.

🛏 **Parrocchia San Giovanni Battista** Ⓞ Do R S 5/50, €Donation, Via Dante Alighieri 7, tel 069 041 094.

🛏 **Case nel Borgo** Ⓞ Pr R K Br W S 3/7, €-/30/60/90, Via di Sant'Andrea 65, casenelborgo@casenelborgo.it, tel 331 600 4982 or 338 286 8402.

STAGE 17
Campagnano di Roma to La Storta

Start	Campagnano di Roma, Piazza Cesare Leonelli
Finish	La Storta, Cathedral of the Sacred Hearts
Total distance	24.2km (less 1.3km with optional shortcut)
Total ascent	559m
Total descent	669m
Difficulty	Moderate
Duration	6¾hr
Percentage paved	53%
Accommodation	Formello 8.8km, La Storta 24.2km

Today's stage goes through portions of the Parco Veio in the Sorbo Valley, lingering among forests and pastures on the way to the outer suburbs of the Eternal City. As the VF's last charming and historic town before Rome, Formello allows intermediate refreshment or a potential overnight, which may be preferable since pilgrims will find La Storta to be a somewhat disappointing and charm-free, car-oriented suburb of Rome. A shortcut option can shave 1.8km off the day just before Isola Farnese.

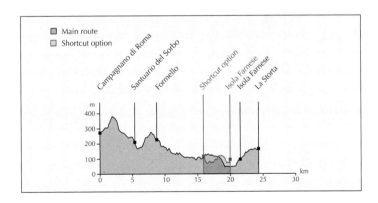

From Piazza Leonelli, continue out the main pedestrian street, Corso Vittorio Emmanuel, heading through the Porta Romana city gates and forking left. Now you are on the **SP10a** roadway, heading slightly uphill and out of town. When the road curves left at the **soccer pitch**, take instead an asphalt road going straight on. Fork right after a fountain and rest area (**1.5km**) and continue more steeply to climb, following signs that lead to Santuario del Sorbo. At a left fork, begin downhill, coming to a narrow asphalt road, the **Strada delle Pastine** (**1.7km**) near the Sorbo Valley floor where you turn left among olive orchards and small pastures. After a short time, the route forks left onto **Strada del Sorbo**, where a sign announces you have entered **Parco Veio**, the setting for much of the day's walk. The 15,000 hectare Parco Veio was established by the Region of Lazio in 1997 as part of a plan to preserve a greenbelt of natural and agricultural areas around urban Rome. The name derives from the Etruscan city of Veius near present-day Isola Farnese.

As you enter a forest you begin to catch glimpses of a church steeple. When the route makes a hard right turn, you can visit the **Santuario del Sorbo** by going straight ahead and climbing a few steps uphill to the entrance (**2.1km**).

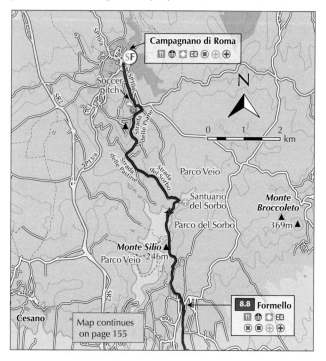

Map continues on page 155

Legends say that in a **visitation** at this serene site the Virgin Mary miraculously regrew a local farmer's withered hand. In the 15th c. Cardinal Orsini constructed a church and convent in honor of the vision over ruins of a 10th c. castle. Above the church's altar is an 11th icon of the Virgin and child and on the apse is a colorful fresco of the assumption of Mary into heaven.

After visiting the sanctuary, return to the route and follow it as it descends deeper into the forested valley. Coming to the valley floor, cross the Cremera Torrente on a small **bridge** and then cross a cattle grid onto a wide, gravel road leading into open pasture land where you may find yourself among horses and cows quietly grazing. You'll also see a marble monument declaring 36km to Rome, erected by the VF confraternity of Formello.

After an arched, steel sculpture on the left the road begins to climb steeply on asphalt, crossing a second steel cattle grid and merging with another asphalt road at the top of the hill. A gathering of houses shows you are very near town – follow signs down to the main traffic street of **Formello**. Continue to follow Via Umberto I with its bars and stores and then, as the road makes a left turn, instead fork right into a small piazza. Here cross under a gate leading to the narrow streets of the town's historic center (**3.4km**).

8.8KM FORMELLO (ELEV 221M, POP 13,113) 🍴 ⊕ 🏧 🅒 ⊙ ⊙ ⊕ ⊕ (34.6KM)

This car-focused Roman commuter town is saved by its quaint and car-free medieval quarter, which is the last picturesque pedestrian neighborhood on the Via Francigena before Rome. The town's three most notable buildings are the 12th c. **Church of San Michele Arcangelo** (open only for special occasions), the 11th c. **Church of San Lorenzo** and the adjacent 11th c. **Palazzo Chigi**, which houses an archeological museum and pilgrim hostel which are reached by glass stairs that recount the journey from Canterbury to Rome on the Via Francigena.

🛏 Ostello Maripara Ⓞ Ⓓⓞ Ⓡ Ⓑⓕ Ⓦ Ⓢ Ⓩ 2/16, €20/-/-/-, Piazza San Lorenzo 3, formaecultura@gmail.com, 069 019 4236. Glass steps here are emblazoned with names of Via Francigena cities.

🛏 Il Palazzetto sulla Francigena Ⓞ Ⓟⓡ Ⓡ Ⓚ Ⓑⓕ Ⓢ 2/4, €-/-/65/-, Via Nazario Sauro 30, ilpalazzetto30@gmail.com, tel 333 789 5953. Detached house.

🛏 Il Rosciolo sulla Francigena Ⓞ Ⓟⓡ Ⓡ Ⓚ Ⓑⓕ Ⓢ 1/4, €-/-/60/-, Via del Rosciolo 3, ilrosciolo3@gmail.com, tel 333 789 5953.

Pilgrims walk through Parco Veio after Formello

Follow the central street of the compact old town as it descends among charming old stone and stucco homes. Take the steep stairways and ramps down toward the gravel road at the valley floor where you reenter Parco Veio. After descending very steeply the gravel road ends and you fork left to climb a dirt road into the woods. The road becomes a path alongside a field of alfalfa and after a time you cross over to the right side of the pastures among bamboo trees again to follow the path. When the path ends at an asphalt road, turn left. Head up the asphalt road, and partway up the hill, take the **gravel road** that forks to the right. A series of asphalt roads now leads you past a tall **sports complex** and onto a bridge across the **SR2bis** Via Veientana Nuova autostrada (**5.2km**).

Go straight ahead after the bridge onto a narrow asphalt road that soon turns to gravel and makes a hard right turn, starting a climb on broken asphalt and concrete. After a tall hedge on the right and **sheep pastures** on the left, watch carefully for a poorly marked left turn onto a gravel road. The road descends for a time and as it begins to climb you come to the Veio shortcut option (**1.8km**), where a right turn offers a 1.3km shorter route to Isola Farnese, bringing you alongside Etruscan archeological sites and an ancient mill before rejoining the main route just after medieval Isola Farnese. The longer, official route carries straight ahead and follows quiet roads, offering views toward Rome, then curving back toward Isola Farnese where it ends at the foot of 13th c. **Castello Farnese**. To access the castle, turn right below the castle wall and then left on the street that climbs the hill into the historic village at the castle gate. The two routes rejoin (**5.6km** official route or **4.3km** via shortcut) just after the castle, at the steep climb on asphalt up to modern, car-centric **Isola Farnese** (**0.9km**).

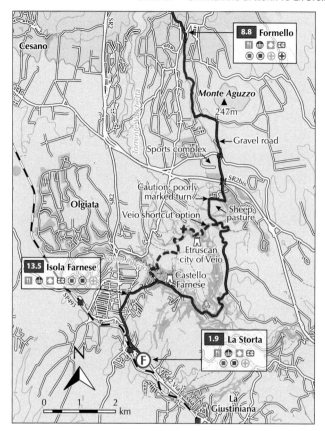

13.5KM ISOLA FARNESE (ELEV 141M, POP 3908)
🍴 ⊕ 🛏 🅒 ◉ ◉ ⊕ (21.1 KM)

The center of modern Isola Farnese is a nondescript, disappointing commercial cluster set where the Via Cassia meets the Via dell'Isola Farnese. Medieval Isola Farnese, easily missed by walkers, is a cluster of buildings around the **castle** (now a wedding venue, www.castellofarnese.it) and the 15th c. **Church of San Pancrazio**, notable for its abundant and lavish frescoes. Historians believe the

15th c. castle, built by the powerful Orsini family, was surrounded by a moat, earning the town the name Isola (tr. 'island'). The town/'island' ultimately was sold to the House of Farnese and carries its name. (Bus and train: see La Storta.)

⌂ **Ostello di Apollo** Ⓞ Ⓟⓣ Ⓡ Ⓑⓡ Ⓓⓡ Ⓖ Ⓢ Ⓩ 15/40, €-/58/83/108, Loc. La Storta, Piazza della Colonnetta 8, info@tempiodiapollo.com, tel 063 089 0595. Inside the castle walls.

Continue left on sidewalks along the Via Cassia to La Storta, which has no true city center, but seems to be just another wide place on this busy road (**1.9km**).

1.9KM LA STORTA (ELEV 166M, POP 18,594) Ⓣⓣ ⊕ ⬠ Ⓒ ◉ ◉ ⊕ (19.2KM)

The name La Storta (tr: 'the twist') likely refers to a series of curves in this stretch of the Via Cassia. Though its San Giovanni church (now disappeared) at Mile IX of the Via Cassia is identified as Sigeric's Stage I Sce Giovanni VIII out of Rome, it is more famous in history as site of an important vision of St Ignatius. In 1537 the founder of the Jesuit order stopped at a small church here where he had a vision of Christ saying, 'I will be favorable to you in Rome.' He feared the vision portended martyrdom, but instead he was warmly welcomed by Pope Paul III. Remembering Christ in his vision, Ignatius determined that his order would be called 'The Society of Jesus,' shortened to 'Jesuits.' The chapel, site of the vision, has been restored and can be viewed at the **Piazza della Visione**. La Storta celebrates the event with a local festival each year on the second Sunday of November. (Bus: frequent departures to Rome on www.atac.roma.it. Train: 3 times hourly departures to Rome at nearby La Storta/Formello station, www.trenitalia.com.)

⌂ **Istituto Suore Poverelle** Ⓓⓞ Ⓡ 4/25, €15/-/-/-, Via Baccarica 5, lastorta@istituto-palazzolo.it, tel 063 089 0495. Summer only.

▲ **Base Scout La Valletta** Ⓡ campground, €Donation, Via della Storta 783, info@basescoutlavalletta.it, online reservations at **www.basescoutlavalletta.it**.

STAGE 18

La Storta to Vatican City

Start	La Storta, Cathedral of the Sacred Hearts
Finish	Vatican City, St Peter's Square
Total distance	19.2km
Total ascent	409m
Total descent	550m
Difficulty	Moderate
Duration	5½hr
Percentage paved	80%
Accommodation	Rome 19.2

After a walk on sidewalks of the Via Cassia, this final stage avoids industrial areas and instead passes through the green and serene La Insugherata Nature Reserve, a peaceful respite amidst otherwise busy city streets and arterial roads. After a few kilometers of suburban sidewalks, the itinerary then finds a second oasis of quiet in Monte Mario Park, with its dramatic views over Rome and Vatican City. The trials and ordeals of the last days and weeks are forgotten as Viale Angelico draws you closer to Piazza San Pietro and the Vatican's grand and glorious Basilica San Pietro.

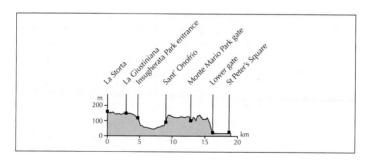

Thread your way along the Via Cassia through the parked cars of commercial La Storta and follow the often-busy highway on the left or right side, depending on the availability of sidewalks. To skip the roadside walk, take bus Urbana #201 'Mancini' from La Storta along the Via Cassia to the Barbarano/Romano stop

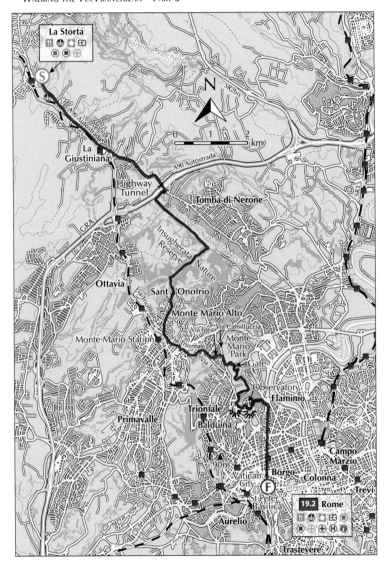

before the entrance to Insugherata Reserve (€1.50 www.atac.roma.it, 48 departures daily). Pass a handy supermarket on the right and find more services as you reach the sprawling **La Guistiniana** neighborhood with its occasional bars and small shops. Just after crossing above the **A90 Autostrada** motorway tunnel, turn right and pass through the gates of the **Insugherata Nature Reserve (4.7km)**, your home for the next hour.

> The **Riserva Naturale dell'Insugherata** is an undeveloped park that encompasses the watershed of the Acqua Traversa stream. Its rich riparian environment is home to cork oak (Italian: *insughera*) and many other native species of plants and animals. The floor of the wide canyon even hosts flocks of sheep, although the area is just at the fringe of the apartments and cars of suburban Rome.

Walk down the asphalt drive and turn left, soon coming to a dirt path alongside the **Acqua Traversa** stream at the floor of the canyon, with apartment blocks occasionally visible on either ridge. After a time the path turns right and, when it passes a gravel road at a white gate, climbs steeply up into the Roman residential neighborhood of **Sant'Onofrio (4.3km**, cafés). In two blocks turn left onto Via Achille Mauri which curves downhill to the **Via Trionfale (1.2km**, cafés), one of Rome's historic main arterial roads. Turn left and follow the Trionfale past businesses, crossing a complex intersection to the other side of the street and staying on it until VF signs point you left onto **Via Igea (1.7km**, cafés).

Follow this road among storefront shops until just before it ends in a couple of blocks. Turn right onto the **Via della Camilluccia** and continue another two blocks until signs point you downhill on a two-lane road where you find the first gate (**0.9km**) of the **Monte Mario Park**. Climb the trail here, sometimes steep and rutted, and enjoy your first vistas over the northern neighborhoods of Rome. Descend and climb again for a second vista, then skirt alongside a metal fence that surrounds the **Astronomical Observatory of Rome** and find yourself back at the Via Trionfale (**1.9km**), now a quieter arterial road.

Walk 50m downhill and reenter the Monte Mario Park, following footpaths 200m to the first viewpoint (**2.1km**) over the southern neighborhoods of the City of Rome and catching your first vista of the majestic dome of St Peter's Basilica. After relishing your accomplishment and enjoying the beauty of the white marble city set among green hills, continue on the rough, cobblestone path as it descends on switchbacks to the lower gate of the park. Go two blocks straight ahead and turn right on a wide and green boulevard, the **Viale Angelico (1.9km**, cafés), a commercial arterial road which you follow for just over 2km, passing the tall **Vatican City** walls and coming to the colonnade of **St Peter's Square** at the foot of **St Peter's Basilica**.

19.2KM ROME (ELEV 26M, POP 2.9 MILLION)
🚪 ⊕ ⌂ Ⓒ ⊙ ⊚ ⊕ ⊕ Ⓗ ❶ (0.0KM)

Few events in life compare to the joy of arriving on foot at St Peter's Square in Rome. Surrounding you are the 140 statues of popes, martyrs, evangelists and saints carved by Bernini and his students. Ahead of you is mighty St Peter's Basilica, still after 500 years the largest church building in the world at an astounding 15,000m². Behind you are the monuments of ancient Rome – the Colosseum, the Pantheon, the Forum – religious Rome – the major and minor basilicas and 900-odd other churches – and modern Rome – the wedding cake-like Victor Emmanuel II Monument, the Spanish Steps, the parks and museums. Rome is also a network of human-scale neighborhoods, like Trastevere, Capo de'Fiori and the Ghetto. It is a city of 2000 fountains, 50 of them of monumental scale. It is a political hub, serving as the capital of the Republic of Italy and the Region of Lazio. It is religious center of the 1.2 billion-member Roman Catholic Church. It is a treasure of sights and sounds, tastes and smells, all with a distinctly Roman-Italian bustle, chaos and flair.

Receiving your Testimonium

The easiest way to receive your Testimonium completion certificate is to go to the St Peter's Square office of the **Opera Romana Pellegrinaggi**. With your back to St Peter's, walk past the colonnade to the ground floor of a five-story yellow-brick building immediately adjacent on the right. Look for the 'Meeting Point' sign where you'll find the office (Mon–Sat 09:00–17:00, Sun/holidays 09:00–13:00, www.omnivaticanrome.org). Present your stamped credential here and the busy staff, which mostly serves tourists and bus pilgrims, will give you your Testimonium. Local Italians and VF stewards are working to make the business-like reception here more hospitable. Though more difficult (no backpacks allowed inside), it is possible to receive your Testimonium inside **St Peter's Basilica** itself, in the Sacristy just off the left transept. Your credential is required for access, and often the staff in the Sacristy (closed daily 13:00–16:00) are nervous about writing out credentials since they usually are not English speakers. They do keep a supply in their desk, however, and have a lovely stamp for your credential whether or not you can talk a Testimonium out of them. You could also ask the Swiss Guards on the left side of the basilica for a security pass to secure your Testimonium at the offices of the **Rectory** (backpacks not allowed).

Seeing the Vatican

In St Peter's Square, don't miss the 4000-year-old Egyptian obelisk right in the middle, which was brought to Rome by the Emperor Caligula in 37 AD to grace his Roman Circus, which stood to the left of the current basilica. Moving the obelisk undamaged in the 16th c. to its present location took over a year. The two

Early morning light finds a quiet St Peter's Square in Rome

17th c. Moderno and Bernini fountains are themselves works of art, as is Bernini's grand, oval colonnade with 140 statues above. Entrance to the most important monument of the Vatican City, **St Peter's Basilica**, is free and well worth the wait in the long line for security checks (backpacks not allowed). Just after entering, look to the far right behind glass for Michelangelo's Pietà, one of the world's most revered sculptures and one of its most emotive. Back in the central nave, find the 13th c. statue of St Peter by Arnolfo di Cambio, where the caresses of millions of pilgrims have nearly rubbed off the saint's bronze toes. Turn left to see the monumental baldachin of Bernini, the bronze canopy directly under Michelangelo's dome and above the Tomb of St Peter. To the left of the baldachin is the Tomb of Pope Alexander VII, the last work designed by the 17th c. sculptor Bernini. A tour of the astounding **Vatican Museum** is worth as much time as you can spare to explore the 54 galleries displaying over 20,000 works of ancient to modern sculpture, painting and tapestries (€14–17, www.museivaticani.va, always book online). Last stop on the museum visit is the **Sistine Chapel**, with its justly renowned frescoes by Michelangelo. Morning is a great time to climb to the top of the **dome** of St Peter's where you can enjoy the best view of the Eternal City. (€8–10, 08:00–17:00 offseason, 08:00–18:00 Apr–Sept. Tickets are sold at the window after security and before the basilica entrance. Not advised for those with a fear of heights).

Two members of the Swiss Guard stand in a driveway near St Peter's Basilica

Touring Rome

Seeing even the major sites of Rome would take several days. A touristic high-light walk would begin at **Piazza Navona**, heading on foot to the **Pantheon**, the Roman-era dome that was a model for many successive domes around the world. Whet your retail appetite by walking north among the stores on the nearby Via del Corso, turning right at the Via delle Muratte to visit **Trevi Fountain**. After casting a coin into the fountain head north again, following signs to Piazza di Spagna and the **Spanish Steps**, a favorite snapshot, gelato and people-watching hangout. From there head north on the Via del Bauino to **Piazza del Popolo** to see the Caravaggios at Santa Maria del Popolo. Spend the evening at a restaurant in **Trastevere** and enjoy one of Rome's most beloved neighborhoods – you've earned yourself a special dinner to celebrate the joys and hardships you've encountered as you've walked one of the world's great pilgrim trails.

Ponte Sant'Angelo spans the Tiber River in Rome with Castel Sant'Angelo in the background

⛪ Ostello Villa Monte Mario ⭕ Pr Do R Br Dr Cf W S Z 48/80, €40/60/-/-, Via Trionfale 6157, info@villamontemario.com, tel 063 540 641 or 334 229 7497. Youth hostel run by Carmelite nuns. Mass 07:00 Mon–Sat, Sun 09:00.

⛪ Spedale della Provvidenza di San Giacomo e San Benedetto Labre ⭕ Do Br Dr W S 2/24, €Donation, Via dei Genovesi 11B, info@pellegriniaroma.it, tel 327 231 9312. Reservations not accepted. Doors open at 15:00. This is Rome's primary pilgrim-focused hostel and is hosted by the beloved Italian confraternity of pilgrims.

⛪ Ostello Marello ⭕ Pr R S 10/14, €-/-/54/-, Via Urbana 50, hostelmarello@yahoo.it, tel 064 882 120 or 064 825 361. Managed by Oblate Sisters of St Joseph.

⛪ Casa per Ferie Centro Pellegrini Santa Teresa Couderc ⭕ Pr R Br Z 50/96, €-/49/74/99, Via Vincente Ambrosio 9/11, groups@centropellegrini.it, tel 063 540 1142 or 340 852 6931.

▲ Cobragor ⭕ Pr R K Cf W S Z 3/11, €-/30/40/50, Via Giuseppe Barellai 60, **www.cobragor.org**, cobragor@gmail.com, tel 063 386 271. Located at coop farm near Insugherata Park.

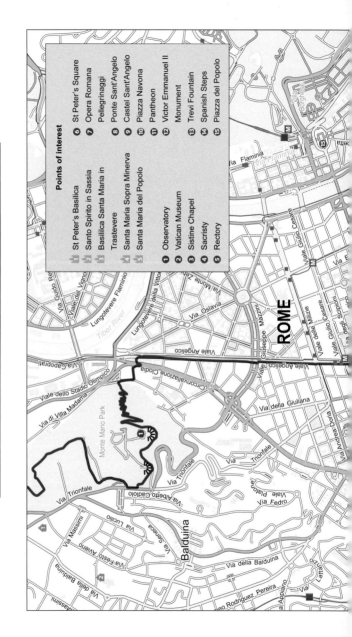

ROME AND VATICAN CITY

Points of interest

1. St Peter's Basilica
2. Santo Spirito in Sassia
3. Basilica Santa Maria in Trastevere
4. Santa Maria Sopra Minerva
5. Santa Maria del Popolo

6. St Peter's Square
7. Opera Romana Pellegrinaggi
8. Ponte Sant'Angelo
9. Castel Sant'Angelo
10. Piazza Navona
11. Pantheon
12. Victor Emmanuel II Monument
13. Trevi Fountain
14. Spanish Steps
15. Piazza del Popolo

1. Observatory
2. Vatican Museum
3. Sistine Chapel
4. Sacristy
5. Rectory

ROME

Balduina

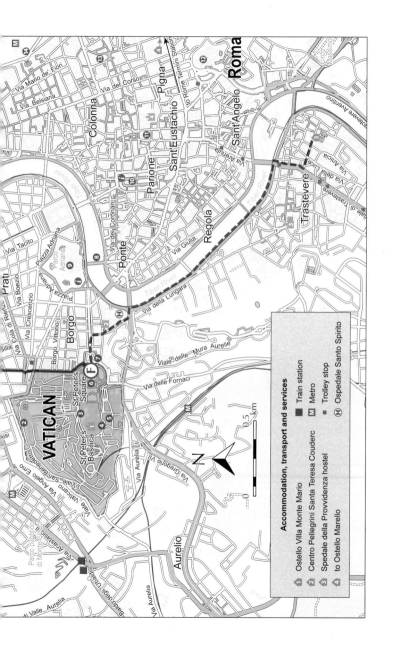

APPENDIX A
Stage planning table

Book stage no.	Location	Distance from start	Distance from previous point	Distance, book stages	My itinerary
1	Lucca	0.0	0.0		
	Capannori	6.6	6.6		
	Badia Posseverie	16.4	9.8		
2	Altopascio	18.3	1.9	18.3	
	Galleno	26.0	7.7		
	Ponte a Cappiano	32.6	6.6		
	Fucecchio	37.6	5.0		
	San Miniato Basso	44.3	6.7		
3	San Miniato	47.0	2.7	28.7	
	Ostello Sigerico	70.1	23.1		
4	Gambassi Terme	71.1	1.0	24.1	
5	San Gimignano	84.8	13.7	13.7	
	Colle Val d'Elsa	97.2	12.4		
	Abbadia Isola	108.5	11.3		
6	Monteriggioni	112.2	3.7	27.4	
7	Siena	132.7	20.6	20.6	
	Isola d'Arbia	142.6	9.9		
	Ponte a Tressa	145.0	2.4		
8	Ponte d'Arbia	158.6	13.6	25.9	
	Buonconvento	163.1	4.4		
	Torrenieri	177.2	14.1		
9	San Quirico d'Orcia	184.8	7.6	26.2	
	Agriturismo Passalacqua	201.7	16.9		
10	Radicofani	217.7	16.0	32.9	
	Ponte a Rigo	228.2	10.5		
	Centeno	232.9	4.7		
11	Acquapendente	240.8	8.0	23.1	
	San Lorenzo Nuovo	252.0	11.2		

12	Bolsena	264.2	12.0	23.2
13	Montefiascone	280.5	16.4	16.4
14	Viterbo	298.6	18.1	18.1
15	Vetralla	315.4	16.8	16.8
	Capranica	331.8	16.4	
16	Sutri	339.4	7.6	24.0
	Monterosi	352.4	13.0	
17	Campagnano di Roma	367.1	14.7	27.7
	Formello	375.9	8.8	
	Isola Farnese	389.5	13.5	
18	La Storta	391.3	1.9	24.2
	St Peter's Square	410.5	19.2	19.2
		Average distance/day		20.9

APPENDIX B
Useful contacts

Italian emergency phone numbers
- 112 Carabinieri (national police and general emergency number)
- 113 State police (theft, robbery, assaults, accidents and health emergencies)
- 115 Fire department
- 117 Finance police
- 118 Medical emergencies
- 1515 Forest fires

Baggage services
SloWays €15 per stage per bag, priced per official stages. More details at www.sloways.eu/luggage-transfer-via-francigena, or reserve at info@sloways.eu.
BagsFree (€20, https://bags-free.com/francigena-luggage-transport. Daily pick-up is by 08:30 each day with delivery by 15:00. BagsFree also offers a baggage storage service near Rome's Termini train station (www.bags-free.com) and can deliver your bags to your hotel from storage.
Via-Francigena-Viterbo-Roma Baggage transport from Viterbo to Rome (www.viafrancigena-viterbo-roma.it), at €40 per stage minimum for up to 4 bags.

Acquire your credential at these locations
Lucca:
Via Francigena Entry Point of Lucca, Via dei Bacchettoni 8 (near Porta Elisa)
Lucca Tourist Office, Vecchia Porta San Donato, Piazzale Verdi
Tourist Center of Lucca, Piazzale Ricasoli 203
Museo della Cattedrale of Lucca, Piazza Antelminelli 5
Capannori:
Ostello 'La Salana' of Capannori, Via del Popolo 182
Fucecchio:
Nuovo Teatro Pacini in Fucecchio, Piazza Montanelli
Fondazione San Miniato Promozione, Piazza del Popolo 1
San Miniato:
Pro Loco of San Miniato, Piazza del Popolo 31
Gambassi Terme:
Tourist Office, Via Volterrana 60
San Gimignano:
Associazione Pro Loco of San Gimignano, Piazza Duomo 1
Colle di Val d'Elsa:
Tourist Office of Colle di Val d'Elsa, Via del Castello 33

Monteriggioni:
Monteriggioni Tourist Office, Piazza Roma 23
Siena:
Bookshop of Santa Maria della Scala in Siena, Piazza Duomo 1
San Quirico d'Orcia:
Palazzo del Pellegrino, Via Dante Alighieri 33
Radicofani:
Tourist office and pilgrim's shop, Via Fonte Antese
Acquapendente:
Centro Informazioni del Pellegrino, Via Ruganella
Centro Visite, Via Torre Julia de Jacopo
Viterbo:
Tourist Office of Viterbo, Piazza Martiri d'Ungheria
Bistrot Caffeina of Viterbo, Via Cavour 9
Sutri: Platea Cavour Casavacanze, Piazza Cavour 12 (by appointment)
Campagnano di Roma:
Mediterraid Cammina Association, Via S. Andrea 66 (by appointment)

Tourist information offices
Lucca:
Vecchia Porta San Donato, and Piazzale Verdi, tel 0583 583 150, info@luccaitinera.it
San Miniato:
Piazza del Popolo, tel 057 142 745, www.sanminiatopromozione.com/en
Gambassi Terme:
Via Volterrana, tel 0571 639 006, turismo@comune.gambassi-terme.fi.it
Colle di Val d'Elsa:
Via del Castello, tel 0577 922 791, turisticocolle@tiscali.it
Monteriggioni:
Piazza Roma, tel 0577 304 834, info@monteriggioniturismo.it
Siena:
Il Campo, tel 331 742 2646 or 331 746 4277, sienatourism@gmail.com
Radicofani:
SP24 Via Fonte Antese, tel 331 529 1556 / 057 855 684, infostelloradicofani@libero.it
Bolsena:
Piazza Matteotti, tel 076 179 9923, ufficioturistico@comune.bolsena.vt.it, www.visitbolsena.it
Montefiascone:
Piazza Vittorio Emanuele, visit@comune.montefiascone.vt.it, www.visitmontefiascone.it
Viterbo:
Piazza Martiri d'Ungheria, tel 0761 226427, www.promotuscia.it
Rome:
Via della Conciliazione, tel 066 988 3566, www.turismoroma.it/info-viaggio

APPENDIX C
Bibliography

Travelogues

Belloc, Hillare. *The Path to Rome.* New York: Wallachia, 1953.

Bucknall, Harry. *Like a Tramp, Like a Pilgrim: On Foot, Across Europe to Rome.* London: Bloomsbury Continuum, 2014.

Egan, Timothy. *A Pilgrimage to Eternity: From Canterbury to Rome in Search of a Faith.* New York: Viking, 2019.

Muirhead, Robert. *The Long Walk: A Pilgrimage from Canterbury to Rome.* CreateSpace, 2015.

Warrender, Alice, *An Accidental Jubilee: A Pilgrimage on foot from Canterbury to Rome.* York: Stone Trough Books, 2011.

Historical – Via Francigena

Caselli, Giovanni. *Via Romea, Cammino di Dio.* Florence: Giunti Gruppo Editoriale, 1990.

Champ, J. *The English Pilgrimage to Rome.* Herfordshire, UK: Gracewing, 2000.

Magoun, F.P. 'The Rome of Two Northern Pilgrims: Archbishop Sigeric of Canterbury and Abbot Nikolas of Munkathvera.' *The Harvard Theological Review*, 33(4), 267–289.

Ortenberg, Veronica. 'Archbishop Sigeric's Journey to Rome in 990.' In M. Lapidge, M. Godden, & S. Keyes (eds.) *Anglo-Saxon England* , Vol 19. (pp.19–26) Cambridge, UK: Cambridge University Press, 1990. Ortenberg studies the meaning of the 23 churches visited by Sigeric in Rome.

Historical – Italy, pilgrimage and general

Birch, Debra J. *Pilgrimage to Rome in the Middle Ages.* Woodbridge, Suffolk: Boydell Press, 1998.

Gilmour, David. *The Pursuit of Italy: A History of a Land, its Regions, and their Peoples.* New York: Farrah, Strauss and Giroux, 2011.

Webb, Diana. *Pilgrims and Pilgrimage in the Medieval West.* London: I.B. Tauris, 2001.

Scotti, R. A. *Basilica: The Splendor and the Scandal, Building St Peter's.* New York: Plume, 2007.

APPENDIX D
Sigeric's journey: then and now

Stage no. from English Channel to Rome	Sigeric's stage no. from Rome to English Channel	Sigeric's place name	Modern place name	Guidebook stage no.
Via Francigena Part 1: Canterbury to Lausanne				
1	LXXX	Sumeran	Sombre (Wissant)	
2	LXXIX	Unlisted by Sigeric		
3	LXXVIII	Gisne	Guînes	
4	LXXVII	Teranburh	Thérouanne	
5	LXXVI	Bruwaei	Bruay-la-Buissière	
6	LXXV	Atherats	Arras	
7	LXXIV	Duin	Doingt	
8	LXXIII	Martinwaeth	Séraucourt-le-Grand	
9	LXXII	Mundlothuin	Laon	
10	LXXI	Corbunei	Corbeny	
11	LXX	Rems	Reims	
12	LXIX	Chateluns	Châlons-sur-Marne	
13	LXVIII	Funtaine	Fontaine-sur-Coole	
14	LXVII	Domaniant	Donnement	
15	LXVI	Breone	Brienne-la-Vieille	
16	LXV	Bar	Bar-sur-Aube	
17	LXIV	Blaecuile	Blessonville	
18	LXIII	Oisma	Humes-Jorquenay	
19	LXII	Grenant	Grenant	
20	LXI	Sefui	Seveux	
21	LX	Cuscei	Cussey-sur-l'Ognon	
22	LIX	Bysiceon	Besançon	
23	LVIII	Nos	Nods	
24	LVII	Punterlin	Pontarlier	
25	LVI	Antifern	Yverdon-les-Bains	
26	LV	Urba	Orbe	

Stage no. from English Channel to Rome	Sigeric's stage no. from Rome to English Channel	Sigeric's place name	Modern place name	Guidebook stage no.
Via Francigena Part 2: Lausanne to Lucca				
27	LIV	Losanna	Lausanne	
28	LIII	Vivaec	Vevey	
29	LII	Burbulei	Aigle	
30	LI	Sancte Maurici	Saint-Maurice	
31	L	Ursiores	Orsières	
32	XLIX	Petrecastel	Bourg-Saint-Pierre	
33	XLVIII	Sancte Remei	Saint-Rhémy	
34	XLVII	Agusta	Aosta	
35	XLVI	Publei	Pont-Saint-Martin	
36	XLV	Everi	Ivrea	
37	XLIV	Sancte Agatha	Santhià	
38	XLIII	Vercel	Vercelli	
39	XLII	Tremel	Tromello	
40	XLI	Pamphica	Pavia	
41	XL	Sancte Cristine	Santa Cristina e Bissone	
42	XXXIX	Sancte Andrea	Corte San Andrea	
43	XXXVIII	Placentia	Piacenza	
44	XXXVII	Floricum	Fiorenzuola d'Arda	
45	XXXVI	Sanctae Domnine	Fidenza (called Borgo San Donino until 1927)	
46	XXXV	Mezane	Costamezzana	
47	XXXIV	Philemangenur	Fornovo di Taro	
48	XXXIII	Sancte Moderanne	Berceto	
49	XXXII	Sancte Benedicte	Montelungo	
50	XXXI	Puntremel	Pontremoli	
51	XXX	Aguilla	Aulla	
52	XXIX	Sancte Stephane	Santo Stefano di Magra	
53	XXVIII	Luna	Sarzana (Luni)	
54	XXVII	Campmaior	Camaiore	

		Via Francigena Part 3: Lucca to Rome (current volume)		
55	XXVI	Luca	Lucca	1
56	XXV	Forcri	Porcari	1
57	XXIV	Aqua Nigra	Ponte a Cappiano	2
58	XXIII	Arne Blanca	Fucecchio	2
59	XXII	Sce Dionisii	San Genesio near San Miniato	3
60	XXI	Sce Peter Currant	Coiano (Castelfiorentino)	3
61	XX	Sce Maria Glan	Santa Maria a Chianni (near Gambassi Terme)	3
62	XIX	Sce Gemiane	San Gimignano	4
63	XVIII	Sce Martin in Fosse	San Martino Fosci (Molino d'Aiano)	5
64	XVII	Aelse	Gracciano (Pieve d'Elsa)	5
65	XVI	Burgenove	Badia an Isola (Abbadia d'Isola)	5
66	XV	Seocine	Siena	6
67	XIV	Arbia	Ponte d'Arbia	7
68	XIII	Turreiner	Torrenieri	8
69	XII	Sce Quiric	San Quirico d'Orcia	8
70	XI	Abricula	Briccole di Sotto	9
71	X	Sce Petir in Pail	San Pietro in Paglia (Voltole)	9–10
72	IX	Aquapendente	Acquapendente	10
73	VIII	Sca Cristina	Bolsena	11
74	VII	Sce Flaviane	Montefiascone	12
75	VI	Sce Valentine	Viterbo (Bullicame)	13
76	V	Furcari	Vetralla (Forcassi)	14
77	IV	Suteria	Sutri	15
78	III	Bacane	Baccano (Campagnano di Roma)	16
79	II	Johannis VIIII	San Giovanni in Nono (La Storta)	17
80	I	Urbs Roma	Roma	18

NOTES

A VIA FRANCIGENA GUIDE IN THREE PARTS

Certified by the Council of Europe as an official Cultural Route, the Via Francigena brings to the modern pilgrim the amazing cultural heritage of five nations – England, France, Switzerland, Italy and the Vatican – and highlights their immense natural beauty and deep, ancient heritage. This guidebook is one of a set of three volumes that covers the route.

Part 1 – From Canterbury to Lausanne
The Via Francigena officially begins at Canterbury Cathedral, crosses the English Channel, then makes its way along French canals, battlefields, farmlands and historic villages to arrive at Lake Geneva in Switzerland.

Part 2 – From Lausanne to Lucca
Continuing from easily accessible Lausanne, the Via Francigena climbs toward the headwaters of the mighty Rhône River before branching off to summit the historic Great Saint Bernard Pass. The route descends the Alps along the Aosta Valley, traveling through the Po River Valley and then crossing the scenic Passo della Cisa into Tuscany. After a few days near the coast, the trail swings inland to Lucca, one of Tuscany's medieval jewels.

Part 3 – From Lucca to Rome
From Lucca to Siena the Via Francigena passes through dazzling Tuscan towns like Lucca, San Gimignano and Siena, the route crosses the Orcia and Paglia Valleys into the volcanic tufa stone ridges and basins of Lazio where the centuries-long rule of the Popes is felt in every village. This amazing pilgrimage ends at one of the world's great treasures – the Eternal City of Rome.

Clouds gather over Lago Bolsena as seen from the Rocca dei Papi in Montefiascone (Stage 13)

Via Francigena Route Key

〰 Part 1 – Canterbury to Lausanne

〰 Part 2 – Lausanne to Lucca

〰 Part 3 – Lucca to Rome

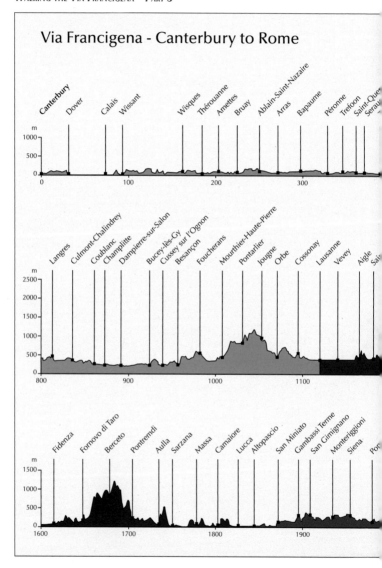

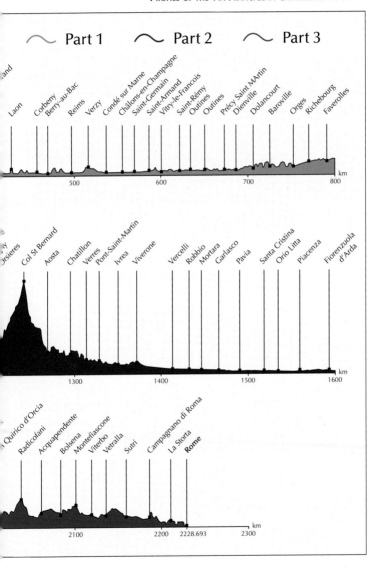

DOWNLOAD THE ROUTES
IN GPX FORMAT

All the routes in this guide are available for download from:

www.cicerone.co.uk/1079/GPX

as GPX files. You should be able to load them into most formats of mobile device, whether GPS or smartphone.

When you go to this link, you will be asked for your email address and where you purchased the guide, and have the option to subscribe to the Cicerone e-newsletter.

www.cicerone.co.uk

LISTING OF CICERONE GUIDES

BRITISH ISLES CHALLENGES, COLLECTIONS AND ACTIVITIES
Cycling Land's End to John o'Groats
The Big Rounds
The Book of the Bivvy
The Book of the Bothy
The C2C Cycle Route
The End to End Cycle Route
The Mountains of England and Wales: Vol 1 Wales
The Mountains of England and Wales: Vol 2 England
The National Trails
Three Peaks, Ten Tors
Walking The End to End Trail

SCOTLAND
Backpacker's Britain: Northern Scotland
Ben Nevis and Glen Coe
Cycle Touring in Northern Scotland
Cycling in the Hebrides
Great Mountain Days in Scotland
Mountain Biking in Southern and Central Scotland
Mountain Biking in West and North West Scotland
Not the West Highland Way
Scotland
Scotland's Best Small Mountains
Scotland's Mountain Ridges
Skye's Cuillin Ridge Traverse
The Ayrshire and Arran Coastal Paths
The Borders Abbeys Way
The Great Glen Way
The Great Glen Way Map Booklet
The Hebridean Way
The Hebrides
The Isle of Mull
The Isle of Skye
The Skye Trail
The Southern Upland Way
The Speyside Way
The Speyside Way Map Booklet
The West Highland Way
The West Highland Way Map Booklet
Walking Highland Perthshire
Walking in Scotland's Far North
Walking in the Angus Glens
Walking in the Cairngorms
Walking in the Ochils, Campsie Fells and Lomond Hills
Walking in the Pentland Hills
Walking in the Scottish Borders
Walking in the Southern Uplands
Walking in Torridon
Walking Loch Lomond and the Trossachs
Walking on Arran
Walking on Harris and Lewis
Walking on Jura, Islay and Colonsay

Walking on Rum and the Small Isles
Walking on the Orkney and Shetland Isles
Walking on Uist and Barra
Walking the Cape Wrath Trail
Walking the Corbetts Vol 1 South of the Great Glen
Walking the Corbetts Vol 2 North of the Great Glen
Walking the Galloway Hills
Walking the Munros Vol 1 – Southern, Central and Western Highlands
Walking the Munros Vol 2 – Northern Highlands and the Cairngorms
Winter Climbs Ben Nevis and Glen Coe
Winter Climbs in the Cairngorms

NORTHERN ENGLAND TRAILS
Hadrian's Wall Path
Hadrian's Wall Path Map Booklet
Pennine Way Map Booklet
The Coast to Coast Map Booklet
The Coast to Coast Walk
The Dales Way
The Dales Way Map Booklet
The Pennine Way

NORTH EAST ENGLAND, YORKSHIRE DALES AND PENNINES
Cycling in the Yorkshire Dales
Great Mountain Days in the Pennines
Mountain Biking in the Yorkshire Dales
St Oswald's Way and St Cuthbert's Way
The Cleveland Way and the Yorkshire Wolds Way
The Cleveland Way Map Booklet
The North York Moors
The Reivers Way
The Teesdale Way
Trail and Fell Running in the Yorkshire Dales
Walking in County Durham
Walking in Northumberland
Walking in the North Pennines
Walking in the Yorkshire Dales: North and East
Walking in the Yorkshire Dales: South and West

NORTH WEST ENGLAND AND THE ISLE OF MAN
Cycling the Pennine Bridleway
Cycling the Way of the Roses
Hadrian's Cycleway
Isle of Man Coastal Path

The Lancashire Cycleway
The Lune Valley and Howgills
Walking in Cumbria's Eden Valley
Walking in Lancashire
Walking in the Forest of Bowland and Pendle
Walking on the Isle of Man
Walking on the West Pennine Moors
Walks in Silverdale and Arnside

LAKE DISTRICT
Cycling in the Lake District
Great Mountain Days in the Lake District
Lake District Winter Climbs
Lake District: High Level and Fell Walks
Lake District: Low Level and Lake Walks
Mountain Biking in the Lake District
Outdoor Adventures with Children – Lake District
Scrambles in the Lake District – North
Scrambles in the Lake District – South
The Cumbria Way
Trail and Fell Running in the Lake District
Walking the Lake District Fells – Borrowdale
Walking the Lake District Fells – Buttermere
Walking the Lake District Fells – Coniston
Walking the Lake District Fells – Keswick
Walking the Lake District Fells – Langdale
Walking the Lake District Fells – Mardale and the Far East
Walking the Lake District Fells – Patterdale
Walking the Lake District Fells – Wasdale

DERBYSHIRE, PEAK DISTRICT AND MIDLANDS
Cycling in the Peak District
Dark Peak Walks
Scrambles in the Dark Peak
Walking in Derbyshire
Walking in the Peak District – White Peak East
White Peak Walks: The Southern Dales

SOUTHERN ENGLAND
20 Classic Sportive Rides in South East England
20 Classic Sportive Rides in South West England

Cycling in the Cotswolds
Mountain Biking on the
  North Downs
Mountain Biking on the
  South Downs
Suffolk Coast and Heath Walks
The Cotswold Way
The Cotswold Way Map Booklet
The Great Stones Way
The Kennet and Avon Canal
The Lea Valley Walk
The North Downs Way
The North Downs Way
  Map Booklet
The Peddars Way and Norfolk
  Coast path
The Pilgrims' Way
The Ridgeway Map Booklet
The Ridgeway National Trail
The South Downs Way
The South Downs Way
  Map Booklet
The South West Coast Path
The South West Coast Path
  Map Booklets
  Vol 1: Minehead to St Ives
  Vol 2: St Ives to Plymouth
  Vol 3: Plymouth to Poole
The Thames Path
The Thames Path Map Booklet
The Two Moors Way
Two Moors Way Map Booklet
Walking Hampshire's Test Way
Walking in Cornwall
Walking in Essex
Walking in Kent
Walking in London
Walking in Norfolk
Walking in the Chilterns
Walking in the Cotswolds
Walking in the New Forest
Walking in the North
  Wessex Downs
Walking in the Thames Valley
Walking on Dartmoor
Walking on Guernsey
Walking on Jersey
Walking on the Isle of Wight
Walking the Jurassic Coast
Walks in the South Downs
  National Park

WALES AND WELSH BORDERS

Cycle Touring in Wales
Cycling Lon Las Cymru
Glyndwr's Way
Great Mountain Days in Snowdonia
Hillwalking in Shropshire
Hillwalking in Wales – Vols 1&2
Mountain Walking in Snowdonia
Offa's Dyke Path
Offa's Dyke Path Map Booklet
Ridges of Snowdonia
Scrambles in Snowdonia

Snowdonia: 30 Low-level and easy
  walks – North
Snowdonia: 30 Low-level and easy
  walks – South
The Cambrian Way
The Ceredigion and Snowdonia
  Coast Paths
The Pembrokeshire Coast Path
The Severn Way
The Snowdonia Way
The Wales Coast Path
The Wye Valley Walk
Walking in Carmarthenshire
Walking in Pembrokeshire
Walking in the Forest of Dean
Walking in the Wye Valley
Walking on the Brecon Beacons
Walking on the Gower
Walking the Shropshire Way

INTERNATIONAL CHALLENGES,
COLLECTIONS AND ACTIVITIES

Canyoning in the Alps
Europe's High Points
The Via Francigena Canterbury to
  Rome – Part 2

AFRICA

Kilimanjaro
The High Atlas
Walking in the Drakensberg
Walks and Scrambles in the Moroccan
  Anti-Atlas

ALPS CROSS-BORDER ROUTES

100 Hut Walks in the Alps
Alpine Ski Mountaineering
  Vol 1 – Western Alps
Alpine Ski Mountaineering Vol 2 –
  Central and Eastern Alps
Chamonix to Zermatt
The Karnischer Hohenweg
The Tour of the Bernina
Tour of Monte Rosa
Tour of the Matterhorn
Trail Running – Chamonix and the
  Mont Blanc region
Trekking in the Alps
Trekking in the Silvretta and
  Ratikon Alps
Trekking Munich to Venice
Trekking the Tour of Mont Blanc
Walking in the Alps

PYRENEES AND FRANCE/SPAIN
CROSS-BORDER ROUTES

Shorter Treks in the Pyrenees
The GR10 Trail
The GR11 Trail
The Pyrenean Haute Route
The Pyrenees
Walks and Climbs in the Pyrenees

AUSTRIA

Innsbruck Mountain Adventures
The Adlerweg
Trekking in Austria's Hohe Tauern
Trekking in the Stubai Alps
Trekking in the Zillertal Alps
Walking in Austria
Walking in the Salzkammergut:
  the Austrian Lake District

EASTERN EUROPE

The Danube Cycleway Vol 2
The High Tatras
The Mountains of Romania
Walking in Bulgaria's National Parks
Walking in Hungary

FRANCE, BELGIUM AND
LUXEMBOURG

Chamonix Mountain Adventures
Cycle Touring in France
Cycling London to Paris
Cycling the Canal de la Garonne
Cycling the Canal du Midi
Mont Blanc Walks
Mountain Adventures in the
  Maurienne
Short Treks on Corsica
The GR20 Corsica
The GR5 Trail
The GR5 Trail – Benelux and Lorraine
The GR5 Trail – Vosges and Jura
The Grand Traverse of the
  Massif Central
The Loire Cycle Route
The Moselle Cycle Route
The River Rhone Cycle Route
The Robert Louis Stevenson Trail
The Way of St James – Le Puy to
  the Pyrenees
Tour of the Queyras
Trekking the Robert Louis
  Stevenson Trail
Vanoise Ski Touring
Via Ferratas of the French Alps
Walking in Corsica
Walking in Provence – East
Walking in Provence – West
Walking in the Ardennes
Walking in the Auvergne
Walking in the Brianconnais
Walking in the Dordogne
Walking in the Haute Savoie: North
Walking in the Haute Savoie: South

GERMANY

Hiking and Cycling in the
  Black Forest
The Danube Cycleway Vol 1
The Rhine Cycle Route
The Westweg
Walking in the Bavarian Alps

HIMALAYA
Annapurna
Everest: A Trekker's Guide
The Mount Kailash Trek
Trekking in Bhutan
Trekking in Ladakh
Trekking in the Himalaya

IRELAND
The Wild Atlantic Way and
    Western Ireland

ITALY
Italy's Sibillini National Park
Shorter Walks in the Dolomites
Ski Touring and Snowshoeing in
    the Dolomites
The Way of St Francis
Trekking in the Apennines
Trekking in the Dolomites
Trekking the Giants' Trail: Alta Via 1
    through the Italian Pennine Alps
Via Ferratas of the Italian Dolomites
    Vols 1&2
Walking and Trekking in the
    Gran Paradiso
Walking in Abruzzo
Walking in Italy's Cinque Terre
Walking in Italy's Stelvio
    National Park
Walking in Sardinia
Walking in Sicily
Walking in the Dolomites
Walking in Tuscany
Walking in Umbria
Walking Lake Como and Maggiore
Walking Lake Garda and Iseo
Walking on the Amalfi Coast
Walking the Via Francigena
    Pilgrim Route – Part 3
Walks and Treks in the
    Maritime Alps

JAPAN, ASIA AND AUSTRALIA
Hiking and Trekking in the Japan Alps
    and Mount Fuji
Hiking the Overland Track
Japan's Kumano Kodo Pilgrimage
Trekking in Tajikistan

MEDITERRANEAN
The High Mountains of Crete
Trekking in Greece
Treks and Climbs in Wadi Rum,
    Jordan
Walking and Trekking in Zagori
Walking and Trekking on Corfu
Walking in Cyprus
Walking on Malta
Walking on the Greek Islands –
    the Cyclades

NORTH AMERICA
The John Muir Trail
The Pacific Crest Trail

SOUTH AMERICA
Aconcagua and the Southern Andes
Hiking and Biking Peru's Inca Trails
Torres del Paine

**SCANDINAVIA, ICELAND
AND GREENLAND**
Trekking in Greenland –
    The Arctic Circle Trail
Trekking in Southern Norway
Trekking the Kungsleden
Walking and Trekking in Iceland
Walking in Norway

**SLOVENIA, CROATIA,
MONTENEGRO AND ALBANIA**
Mountain Biking in Slovenia
The Islands of Croatia
The Julian Alps of Slovenia
The Mountains of Montenegro
The Peaks of the Balkans Trail
The Slovene Mountain Trail
Walking in Slovenia: The Karavanke
Walks and Treks in Croatia

SPAIN AND PORTUGAL
Camino de Santiago:
    Camino Frances
Coastal Walks in Andalucia
Cycle Touring in Spain
Cycling the Camino de Santiago
Mountain Walking in Mallorca
Mountain Walking in
    Southern Catalunya
Portugal's Rota Vicentina
Spain's Sendero Historico: The GR1
The Andalucian Coast to
    Coast Walk
The Camino del Norte and
    Camino Primitivo
The Camino Ingles and Ruta do Mar
The Camino Portugues
The Mountains of Nerja
The Mountains of Ronda
    and Grazalema
The Sierras of Extremadura
Trekking in Mallorca
Trekking in the Canary Islands
Walking and Trekking in the
    Sierra Nevada
Walking in Andalucia
Walking in Menorca
Walking in Portugal
Walking in the Algarve
Walking in the Cordillera Cantabrica
Walking on Gran Canaria
Walking on La Gomera and
    El Hierro

Walking on La Palma
Walking on Lanzarote and
    Fuerteventura
Walking on Madeira
Walking on Tenerife
Walking on the Azores
Walking on the Costa Blanca
Walking the Camino dos Faros

SWITZERLAND
Switzerland's Jura Crest Trail
The Swiss Alpine Pass Route –
    Via Alpina Route 1
The Swiss Alps
Tour of the Jungfrau Region
Walking in the Bernese Oberland
Walking in the Engadine – Switzerland
Walking in the Valais

TECHNIQUES
Fastpacking
Geocaching in the UK
Map and Compass
Outdoor Photography
Polar Exploration
The Mountain Hut Book

MINI GUIDES
Alpine Flowers
Navigation
Pocket First Aid and Wilderness
    Medicine
Snow

MOUNTAIN LITERATURE
8000 metres
A Walk in the Clouds
Abode of the Gods
Fifty Years of Adventure
The Pennine Way – the Path, the
    People, the Journey
Unjustifiable Risk?

For full information on all our guides,
books and eBooks,
visit our website:
www.cicerone.co.uk